YOUNG ADULT ELI READERS **B1**

The ELI Readers collection is a complete
range of book
of all ages, ra
contemporary
There are thre
a different ag
Teen ELI Reac
Readers. The books are carefully edited and beautifully illustrated to capture the essence of the stories and plots.
The readers are supplemented with 'Focus on' texts packed with background cultural information about the writers and their lives and times.

Jane Austen

Pride and Prejudice

Adaptation and activities by Janet Borsbey and Ruth Swan
Illustrated by Giovanni Da Re

YOUNG ADULT ELI READERS

Pride and Prejudice
Jane Austen
Adaptation and activities by Janet Borsbey and Ruth Swan
Illustrated by Giovanni Da Re

ELI Readers
Founder and Series Editors
Paola Accattoli, Grazia Ancillani, Daniele Garbuglia (Art Director)

Eli Editorial Staff
Natalie Bayne

Eli Design Department
Sergio Elisei
Carmen Fragnelli

Production Manager
Francesco Capitano

Photo credits
GettyImages, Shutterstock

A special thanks to all the Team at ELI, E. Chuther, Sarah Howell and Lisa Kester Dodgson

The publisher would like to take this opportunity to thank Sarah Howell for her contribution to the development of the project
The publisher would like to take this opportunity to thank Lisa Kester Dodgson

P.O. Box 6
62019 Recanati MC
Italy
T +39 071750701
F +39 071977851
info@elionline.com
www.elionline.com

Typeset in 11,5 / 15 pt Monotype Dante

Printed in Italy by Tecnostampa Recanati - ERA301.01
ISBN 978-88-536-0504-7

First edition: September 2009

www.elireaders.com

Contents

These icons indicate the parts of the story that are recorded **start** ▶ **stop** ■

MAIN CHARACTERS

Mr and Mrs Bennet live on the Longbourn estate with their five daughters. They are, in order of age, Jane (the eldest), Elizabeth, Mary, Kitty and Lydia.

*Mr Bingley is a rich young man. He has two sisters, **Caroline** and **Louisa**.*

Mr Collins is a clergyman. His patron is Lady Catherine de Bourgh.

*Lady Catherine de Bourgh is Mr Darcy's rich aunt. She has a daughter called **Anne**.*

*Mr Darcy is a rich friend of Mr Bingley's. He has a sister called **Georgiana**.*

Mr Wickham is a handsome soldier from the militia.

Charlotte Lucas is Elizabeth Bennet's best friend.

Word-building

1 a Complete the table with words from the box. Check the meaning in a dictionary if necessary.

~~silliness~~ • excitement • ~~proud~~ • beauty • afraid • beautiful
intelligence • h~~appiness~~ • delighted • ~~prejudiced~~

noun	adjective
happiness	happy
pride	proud
arrogance	arrogant
prejudice	prejudiced
silliness	silly
beauty	beautiful
excitement	excited
delight	delighted
fear	afraid
intelligence	intelligent

1 b Choose the correct alternative in the sentences below. Use the table to check your answers.

1 Jane Bennet was a very *happy/happiness* girl.
2 Everyone agreed that Mr Darcy was very *proud/pride*.
3 People didn't like his *arrogant/arrogance*.
4 The title of this book is 'Pride and *Prejudiced/Prejudice*'.
5 The three younger Bennet sisters were very *silly/silliness*.
6 Everyone admired Jane Bennet's *beautiful/beauty*.
7 There was a lot of *excited/excitement* about the ball.
8 Mrs Bennet was *delighted/delight* that Mr Bingley was rich and single.
9 Elizabeth wasn't *afraid/fear* of Mr Darcy.
10 Mr Darcy liked Elizabeth's *intelligent/intelligence*.

Speaking

2 a Use a dictionary if necessary. Are these adjectives positive (P) or negative (N), or both (B)?

sensitive ___	good-looking ___	polite ___
well-mannered ___	fashionable ___	kind ___
lively ___	clever ___	rude ___
sensible ___	noble ___	rich ___

2 b Work in pairs. Tell each other about people you know who are like this.

Grammar

3 Use the clues below to complete the irregular verb crossword.

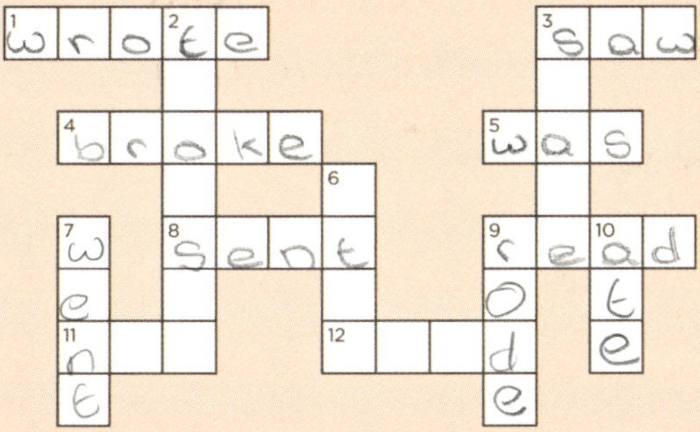

Clues Across

1 Jane _______ a letter to Elizabeth. (5)
3 Mr Darcy _______ Mr Bingley in the distance. (3)
4 When Mr Darcy's pen _______, Caroline offered to mend it. (5)
5 Mr Collins _______ married. (3)
8 Mr Bingley _______ some flowers to Jane. (4)
9 Mary played the piano and Elizabeth _______ her book. (4)
11 Elizabeth _______ Mr Darcy on the road. He gave her a letter.(3)
12 Mr Bennet _______ Mary to stop playing the piano. (4)

Clues Down

2 Mr Collins _______ Elizabeth was very beautiful. (7)
3 Mr Bingley _______ quietly to Jane. (5)
6 Lydia and Kitty _______ to see their aunt. (4)
7 Mr Bingley and Mr Darcy _______ to visit. (4)
9 Mr Darcy got on his horse and _______ away. (4)
10 Lady Catherine _______ a lot of vegetables at dinner. (3)

Chapter One

The Bennets, the Bingleys and Mr Darcy

▶ 2 There is one thing that everybody knows is true. Everybody knows that it is true that any rich, single man must definitely want a wife. And, of course, all mothers think this rich, single man is the perfect partner for one or another of their daughters.

Mr and Mrs Bennet had five daughters and none of them was married, so when rich Mr Bingley came to live at Netherfield Hall, Mrs Bennet was very, very excited.

'Mr Bennet,' she said to her husband one day, 'have you heard? Netherfield Park has been rented at last to a man called Bingley. This is such good news for our girls.'

'Why is that good news for our girls?' replied her husband calmly.

'Oh, Mr Bennet. He's single, he's rich and he's rented Netherfield. He will definitely marry one of our girls. You must go and visit him as soon as you can.'

'No, you go,' he answered, 'Take the girls with you. Then he can choose the girl he likes best.'

Mr Bennet enjoyed teasing* his wife. He knew it was important for him to visit their new neighbour*. If he didn't visit, it would be impossible for his wife and daughters to meet Mr Bingley.

'Oh, Mr Bennet, you are so unkind to your family,' said his wife,

to tease to make fun of

a neighbour a person who lives near you

'Now they'll never get married.'

◈◈◈

A few days later, Mr and Mrs Bennet and their daughters were in their sitting room. Elizabeth, their second daughter, was putting a ribbon* on a hat.

'That's a beautiful hat, Lizzy,' said her father, 'I hope Mr Bingley will like it.'

'We'll never know what Mr Bingley likes,' said Mrs Bennet crossly*, 'We can't visit him.'

Her husband continued speaking. 'When's the next ball in Meryton, Lizzy?' he asked. Meryton was the local village.

'Two weeks tomorrow,' replied Elizabeth happily.

'Oh no! In two weeks!' cried Mrs Bennet, 'Our girls won't be able to dance with Mr Bingley. All the other girls in the village will dance with him. *They* have kind fathers who have visited Mr Bingley.' She paused and looked at Mr Bennet crossly. 'Then he'll marry one of them. He'll marry a girl from the village. I hate the name Bingley already.'

Mr Bennet paused. His eyes were smiling. 'I'm sorry that you hate the name Bingley, my dear, because I visited Mr Charles Bingley today.'

'Oh girls, you have such a kind father! I knew you would visit him! Now you can all dance with Mr Bingley. Oh Jane, Lizzy, Mary, Kitty and Lydia, you have a very kind father!'

Mrs Bennet was overjoyed*. Her husband went into his study to read in peace and quiet. Mrs Bennet and her daughters spent the evening talking about Mr Bingley, Netherfield and the village ball.

◈◈◈

a ribbon a coloured band
crossly angrily
overjoyed very, very happy

The Bennet girls spent the next few days trying to find out about Mr Bingley. Their father had nothing to say about his looks or his personality. In the end, they had to ask their neighbour, Lady Lucas. She described Mr Bingley as young, very good-looking, very pleasant and he liked dancing very much. She had some other exciting news; Mr Bingley was definitely coming to the ball and he was bringing a large group of friends. Lady Lucas's daughter, Charlotte, was Elizabeth's best friend and she was very excited about meeting Mr Bingley and his friends. Mrs Bennet was also very excited. She wasn't a very intelligent woman and she spent a lot of her life thinking about her daughters and their future marriages.

◈◈◈

On the night of the Meryton ball, everyone was already dancing when Mr Bingley arrived. He came with his two sisters, who were very fashionable young women; Caroline, who was single and Louisa, who was married. Louisa's husband was also with them. Another young man was in the group. He was tall and very good-looking. The ladies from the village discovered that his name was Mr Darcy and that he was even richer than Mr Bingley. He had a large estate* in Derbyshire called Pemberley.

Mr Bingley was very popular, he danced with lots of young ladies and he was very kind to everyone. Mr Darcy was not as popular. He only danced with Mr Bingley's sisters and spent a lot of the evening walking around the room. The ladies of Meryton soon agreed that Mr Darcy was very rich, but he was also proud and arrogant.

Mr Bingley was dancing with Jane. He saw his friend watching the dancing. 'Come, Darcy, dance with one of these pretty girls,' he called.

'I hate dancing,' Mr Darcy replied, 'Except for your sisters, you are dancing with the only pretty girl in the room.'

an estate a park with a large house, other small houses and land

'Miss Bennet is the most beautiful girl in the world. But look,' said his friend, pointing to Elizabeth, 'her sister Elizabeth Bennet is also beautiful. She has no-one to dance with.'

'She is quite pretty, I suppose,' replied Darcy coldly, 'but not pretty enough for me. Go back to your partner, go back to Jane Bennet's smiles. Leave me alone.'

Unfortunately for Mr Darcy, Elizabeth heard his comments. She decided that she didn't like Mr Darcy, but she had a good sense of humour. She and her friends were soon laughing about Mr Darcy's behaviour*. The Bennet girls enjoyed the ball. Elizabeth chatted with her good friend Charlotte Lucas and Jane danced with Mr Bingley twice. Kitty and Lydia, the two youngest girls, danced happily all night. Even Mary, who was very serious, seemed to enjoy herself. Mrs Bennet was the happiest of them all; Mr Bingley liked Jane. He was surely going to marry her.

After the ball, Jane and Elizabeth were alone in their room at home. Jane told her sister that she liked Mr Bingley very much. She liked him because he was kind, sensitive, well-mannered and lively. Elizabeth agreed. 'He's also extremely handsome,' she said.

Jane went on to talk about the other people in the group. 'I like his sister, Caroline Bingley. She's coming to live at Netherfield with her brother.'

Elizabeth was not so sure. 'I thought she was quite proud,' said Elizabeth.

◈◈◈

A few days later, the Bennet sisters and their mother visited Caroline Bingley and her sister at Netherfield. After the visit, Caroline and her sister agreed that Jane was a sweet girl. They also agreed that

behaviour the way people act

Mrs Bennet was impossible and that the younger sisters had very bad manners*. Elizabeth still thought that Caroline Bingley was very proud.

◆◆◆

One evening, Sir William Lucas, Charlotte's father, invited the Bennet family to a small party at his house. Mr Bingley, his sisters and Mr Darcy were also there. There was also a group of officers from the militia* who had just arrived in Meryton. They were staying in the village for the winter. After dinner, Mary played some tunes* on the piano. She wasn't very good, but she really enjoyed playing. Jane and Mr Bingley were dancing together and the younger Bennet girls were dancing with some of the officers. Elizabeth and Charlotte Lucas were chatting. Charlotte had noticed that Mr Bingley and Jane seemed to like each other very much. Charlotte thought Jane should tell Mr Bingley that she liked him. She was worried that Jane didn't show her feelings. Mr Darcy was watching Elizabeth. He remembered the ball when he had said she was only *quite* pretty. Now he was looking at her beautiful dark eyes and her intelligent face. He realized he had been wrong, she was very pretty indeed. 'I'd like to get to know her better,' he said to himself. He was a little surprised.

'Miss Elizabeth,' called Sir William Lucas, 'why aren't you dancing? And you Mr Darcy, why don't you dance with this beautiful young lady?'

'Thank you, Sir William, but I don't want to dance,' said Elizabeth very quickly. She was a little embarrassed and not sure what to do. Mr Darcy was very polite. He asked Elizabeth to dance with him. Elizabeth was quite surprised, but she refused politely and walked away.

Caroline Bingley had been watching. She went over to Mr Darcy and whispered, 'I can imagine what you're thinking.'

to have bad manners to be rude or act in a rude way
the militia military men
a tune a piece of music

'What's that?' asked Mr Darcy.

'That it's terrible to spend time with these people. They have such bad manners.'

'Not at all,' replied Mr Darcy, 'I was thinking about Miss Elizabeth Bennet's beautiful dark eyes.'

'I'm very surprised,' said Miss Bingley, who wanted to marry Mr Darcy herself. 'So, Miss Elizabeth Bennet is your favourite. Are you going to marry her? You will have an excellent mother-in-law. Mrs Bennet will be a mother-in-law to be proud of. And she will always be with you at Pemberley.'

Miss Bingley carried on talking. Mr Darcy didn't interrupt her ironic* comments, so soon Miss Bingley felt better. No, Mr Darcy was safe.

Mrs Bennet was determined to find husbands for her daughters for a very good reason. Mr Bennet was not a rich man. He had a very fine house, but a very small income. And there was one big problem; Mr and Mrs Bennet had no sons. When Mr Bennet died, the house and the estate would go to a cousin and not to the Bennet girls. Mrs Bennet's family was not a rich one, so they couldn't help. She had a sister, Mrs Phillips, who lived in Meryton and a brother, Mr Gardiner, who worked in London.

Meryton was about a mile away from Longbourn where the Bennet family lived, so the girls often walked there to visit their aunt. Kitty and Lydia Bennet, however, began to visit Meryton much more often, now that the militia were there. Every time they went to Meryton, they came back with more information about the officers from the militia and their beautiful red coats. Lydia and Kitty were the happiest girls in Longbourn. Their father was not so happy.

ironic saying the opposite of what you really think

'I think you are two of the silliest* girls in England,' he said one day at lunchtime, after listening to them talk about the officers.

Lydia just carried on chatting about Captain Carter and Colonel Forster.

'Silly? Your daughters?' exclaimed Mrs Bennet, 'Not at all. When I was a girl, I liked officers too.'

A servant came into the room with a letter for Jane Bennet. Her mother was delighted*.

'Who's it from? What's it about? What does he say? Come on, Jane, tell us all!' she exclaimed.

'It's from Miss Bingley,' said Jane and she read the letter to her family.

'My dear friend,

You must come for dinner today. The gentlemen are having dinner with the officers, so Louisa and I will be alone. We'll be very bored without your company.

Yours ever,

Caroline Bingley'

'It's a shame* the gentlemen are away,' said Mrs Bennet.

'Can I have the carriage*?' asked Jane.

'No! I think it's going to rain. Take the horse. If it rains, you'll have to stay tonight. Then you'll meet the gentlemen again.'

Jane, Elizabeth and Mr Bennet were all quite shocked.

Soon after Jane left, it started to rain and Mrs Bennet was delighted. It continued to rain all evening and she was sure Jane would stay the night at Netherfield.

silly not intelligent and not serious
delighted very happy
it's a shame it's a pity
a carriage a vehicle pulled by horses

Reading Comprehension

1 Choose the best answer – A, B or C.

1 How many daughters do the Bennets have?
- **A** seven ☐
- **B** three ☐
- **C** five ☒

2 Who is Mr Bingley?
- **A** a rich, married man ☐
- **B** a rich, single man ☒
- **C** a friend of Mr Bennet's ☐

3 Why is Mrs Bennet cross with Mr Bennet?
- **A** because he wants to visit Mr Bingley ☒
- **B** because he is reading his newspaper ☐
- **C** because he doesn't want to visit Mr Bingley ☐

4 What do the ladies of Meryton think about Mr Darcy?
- **A** that he is very proud ☐
- **B** that he is very shy ☐
- **C** that he is very angry ☐

5 What does Mr Darcy say about Elizabeth?
- **A** that she isn't pretty enough for him ☐
- **B** that she is too pretty for him ☐
- **C** that she is a bad dancer ☐

6 What does Mr Bingley think about Jane?
- **A** he likes her very much ☐
- **B** that she isn't as pretty as her sister ☐
- **C** that she is rude ☐

7 Why do Kitty and Lydia start going to Meryton more often than usual?
- **A** to visit Aunt Phillips ☐
- **B** to see the officers ☐
- **C** to see Mr Gardiner ☐

2 Match the characters to the things they say. You can use the characters more than once. Not all characters are used.

1 ☐ 'Mr Bennet, you are so unkind to your family.'
2 ☐ 'I'm sorry you hate the name Bingley, because I visited him today.'
3 ☐ 'I hate dancing. You are dancing with the only pretty girl in the room.'
4 ☐ 'It's terrible to spend time with these people. They have such bad manners.'
5 ☐ 'I think you are two of the silliest girls in England.'
6 ☐ 'Can I have the carriage?'

a Elizabeth Bennet
b Mr Darcy
c Mr Bennet
d Mrs Bennet
e Caroline Bingley
f Jane Bennet
g Mr Bingley
h Charlotte Lucas

PET – Grammar

3 Comparatives. Complete the second sentence so that it means the same as the first, using no more than three words.

1 Mr Bingley isn't as rich as Mr Darcy.
Mr Darcy .... Mr Bingley.

2 Mr Bingley is more popular than Mr Darcy.
Mr Darcy isn't .... Mr Bingley.

3 Elizabeth is less beautiful than Jane.
Jane is .... Elizabeth.

4 Jane is older than Elizabeth.
Elizabeth isn't .... Jane.

5 Pemberley is bigger than Longbourn.
Longbourn isn't .... Pemberley.

4 **Superlatives. Complete the sentences using the superlative form of the adjective in brackets.**

1 Jane is *the most beautiful* girl in the Bennet family. (beautiful)
2 Kitty and Lydia are ______________ Bennet sisters. (silly)
3 Mr Darcy is ______________ man at Netherfield. (proud)
4 Mr Bingley is ______________ man at Netherfield. (kind)
5 Elizabeth is ______________ woman in the village. (intelligent)
6 Charlotte is Elizabeth's ______________ friend. (good)
7 Mrs Bennet is ______________ woman at the ball. (happy)
8 Mary is ______________ piano player at the ball. (bad)

Vocabulary

5 **Choose adjectives from the box to describe the characters in the story. More than one answer is sometimes possible.**

rich • single • kind • young • good-looking • fashionable popular • proud • arrogant • lively • silly • beautiful

Mrs Bennet	Kitty & Lydia	Elizabeth Bennet	Mr Darcy	Mr Bingley	Caroline Bingley

Writing

6 a **Write a dialogue between Jane and Elizabeth.**

Jane: What do you think of Mr Darcy, Elizabeth?
Elizabeth: ______________________________
Jane: Why don't you like him?
Elizabeth: ______________________________
Jane: And, what do you think of Mr Bingley?
Elizabeth: ______________________________
Jane: Oh, I liked him very much too. Did you like his sisters?
Elizabeth: ______________________________
Jane: Really? I don't agree. I liked Caroline Bingley. Why don't you like her?
Elizabeth: ______________________________
Jane: Do you think I'll meet Mr Bingley again? I really like him.
Elizabeth: ______________________________

6 b Either

Imagine that you are Miss Elizabeth Bennet. Write about your first impression of Mr Darcy.

Or

Imagine that you are Mr Darcy. Write about your first impression of Miss Elizabeth Bennet.

PRE-READING ACTIVITIES

PET – Listening

▶ 3 **7 Listen to the beginning of the next chapter. The following morning, a letter came from Jane to Elizabeth. Listen to Lizzy reading the letter and choose the best answer.**

1 Jane is	**A** hot	☐
	B ill	☐
	C tired	☐
2 The reason is	**A** because she got cold	☐
	B because she got wet	☐
	C because she walked a long way	☐
3 Her friends say Jane must	**A** go home immediately	☐
	B go to the ball	☐
	C stay until she is better	☐
4 In the letter Jane tells Lizzy	**A** to come immediately	☐
	B to go to Meryton	☐
	C not to worry	☐
5 Jane has	**A** a sore leg	☐
	B a sore head	☐
	C a sore throat	☐

Speaking

8 Talk in pairs. What do you think happens next?

- Does Elizabeth go to see Jane?
- Does Jane get better?

Chapter Two

Mr Collins Comes to Stay

3 The following morning, a letter came from Jane to Elizabeth.

'My dearest Lizzy,
I don't feel very well this morning. I got wet yesterday. My friends here at Netherfield say I must stay here until I'm better. They have called the doctor. Don't worry, I just have a sore throat and a headache.
Love from your sister,
Jane'

4 Elizabeth read the note to her family and Mr Bennet was the first to speak. 'Well, my dear,' he said to his wife, 'if Jane dies, at least she was doing her duty*, as you asked.'

'Nobody dies of a cold,' replied his wife, 'She can stay at Netherfield until she's better. She will have more time to get to know* Mr Bingley.'

Elizabeth decided to visit her sister at Netherfield. She decided to walk. It was a beautiful day, although the road was very wet and muddy*. Kitty and Lydia walked as far as Meryton with her and then Elizabeth continued to Netherfield alone. It was another two miles. When she arrived, the servant took her to the breakfast room. Mr Bingley's sisters were very surprised when they realised that Elizabeth had walked from Longbourn. They didn't like the fact that her dress was very muddy. Mr Bingley was very kind but Mr Darcy was very

to do your duty to do the right thing
to get to know to become friends with someone
muddy dirty from dirt in a wet field

quiet; he was thinking about her face and her bright eyes. Elizabeth went upstairs to see her sister. As soon as she left the room, Caroline Bingley laughed.

'Did you see her dress?'

'I know, the mud!' replied her sister.

'Well Mr Darcy, do you still admire her fine eyes?' asked Caroline.

'Yes, I do. The walk made them brighter.'

This was not the answer Caroline Bingley had hoped to hear.

◈◈◈

Later, after Elizabeth had seen Jane, Mr Bingley suggested that Elizabeth stay until Jane was better. In the evening, Elizabeth stayed with Jane while the ladies and gentlemen had dinner. Conversation at the dinner table was mainly about the Bennet family.

'Jane Bennet is a sweet girl,' said Caroline, 'but the family is very low. Their uncles don't have estates, they work. They live in a moderate area of London.'

'That's not a problem for me,' cried Mr Bingley, 'I think the Bennet girls are nice and they are beautiful.'

'Yes, but they can't hope to make a good marriage with such low connections,' added Mr Darcy.

Bingley didn't reply.

After dinner, Elizabeth joined them in the dining room, for coffee. Everyone was playing cards, so Elizabeth started to read. Miss Bingley decided to show Elizabeth up*. 'Mr Darcy, do tell me. Is your sister Georgiana as tall as I am, yet?'

'No, she's about Miss Elizabeth Bennet's height,' he replied.

'I really want to see her again,' continued Caroline Bingley, 'She's so clever and so beautiful and she plays the piano so well.'

to show someone up to show someone's bad points

Mr Bingley joined in the conversation. 'All young ladies are so clever. They paint, they draw, they make clothes and all types of things.'

Mr Darcy disagreed. 'I only know six clever women,' he said.

'Yes,' said Caroline Bingley, 'a really clever woman must know a lot about music, singing, drawing and modern languages and she must have an aristocratic air in the way she walks and the way she speaks.'

Of course, Miss Bingley was talking about herself. She thought she was much cleverer than Elizabeth. Mr Darcy then added his opinion. 'Yes, all of that, but in addition, she must read a lot to improve her mind*.'

'I'm surprised you know any clever women,' said Elizabeth, 'I don't know anyone as clever as that!' and she went upstairs to see Jane.

◈◈◈

The following morning, Jane was much better. Just after breakfast, she had a visitor. Mrs Bennet came to see her with Kitty and Lydia. Everyone sat in the morning room. Conversation was very difficult because Mrs Bennet decided to be very rude to Mr Darcy. Elizabeth was embarrassed at her mother's rudeness. She was also embarrassed that Lydia seemed out of control. Kitty behaved the same as Lydia, as usual. The two youngest Bennet girls chatted about the militia and balls. They asked Mr Bingley to hold a ball at Netherfield and he agreed. Eventually, Mrs Bennet, Kitty and Lydia left, leaving Jane and Elizabeth at Netherfield. Caroline Bingley and her sister then gossiped* unkindly about the Bennet family.

The following evenings were very similar to the first evening. Elizabeth thought that Miss Bingley wanted Mr Darcy's attention all the time. When Mr Darcy was writing a letter to his sister, Elizabeth smiled, as Miss Bingley complimented Mr Darcy on his writing; it

a mind intelligence

to gossip to talk about people and their lives, sometimes unkindly

was so fast and so beautiful. Then, Miss Bingley offered to mend his pen when it broke. If everyone was reading a book, Miss Bingley watched Mr Darcy instead of reading her own. One evening, she even invited Elizabeth to walk around the room, so that Mr Darcy could admire her figure. When Elizabeth joked about Mr Darcy's faults, Miss Bingley insisted that he was perfect. 'I have many faults,' replied Mr Darcy, 'I have a bad temper. I'm proud, but I don't think pride is always wrong. I'm quite shy and I don't change my mind. If I have a bad opinion of someone, I never change it.'

'That's terrible,' replied Elizabeth, 'That means you never forgive people.'

'And you pretend* not to understand people,' said Mr Darcy. He was smiling.

Miss Bingley was a little worried. She began to think that Mr Darcy really liked Elizabeth. 'Let's play some music, Louisa,' she said quickly to her sister.

◈◈◈

After a few days, Jane was feeling much better and she and Elizabeth decided to go home to Longbourn. Caroline and Louisa said they were sorry that the Bennet sisters had to go home, but Elizabeth was certain that they were very happy. Mr Darcy was happy that Elizabeth was going home, he was beginning to like her too much. Mr Bingley was very sad. He asked Jane to stay for at least a few more days, but Jane had decided.

Mr Bennet was happy to see the girls back at Longbourn, as the evening conversation had been very boring without them. Mrs Bennet was very irritated. She thought the girls had come home too soon. She had hoped that Mr Bingley would ask Jane to marry him.

to pretend to act differently from the way you really are

Mary was happy because she wanted to talk to them about a book she was reading. Kitty and Lydia were delighted too – they wanted to talk about the militia officers in Meryton. The routine at Longbourn soon continued as normal.

◈◈◈

At breakfast, the next morning, Mr Bennet spoke to his wife. 'I hope dinner will be good, because we'll have a guest.'

'Who, oh who?' asked his wife, excitedly.

'A gentleman and a stranger,' replied Mr Bennet.

'Mr Bingley!' exclaimed Mrs Bennet.

'No, it isn't Mr Bingley. It's a person I have never met before.'

His wife and daughters were very curious. 'It's Mr Collins, my cousin,' he said, 'He's a very important visitor, as he will inherit this house when I die. Before you ask, he'll be here at four o'clock to satisfy your curiosity. I think, however, that he may be a very silly young man.'

◈◈◈

At four o'clock exactly, Mr Collins arrived. He looked extremely serious. He was wearing the typical clothes of a clergyman*. He complimented Mrs Bennet on having five very beautiful daughters. He admired the furniture and the house. He also complimented Mrs Bennet on the cooking. It was very clear, however, that the most important person in his life was his patron*, Lady Catherine de Bourgh. All through dinner, he talked about Lady Catherine, her great house and her daughter. He obviously spent a lot of his time thinking about the great Lady Catherine. 'She is a very great lady,' he said, 'She sometimes drives past my house in her carriage.

a clergyman a priest, a man of the church

a patron a rich person who protects someone

I'm always ready to run out so that I can speak to her. She is proud, from a very noble family, but she often invites me to Rosings Park for dinner. Rosings Park, you understand, is one of the finest country estates in England.'

Mr Bennet and Elizabeth enjoyed listening to Mr Collins because he was indeed very silly. The other members of the family thought he was boring. Jane was very kind to him, because Jane was kind to everyone.

◈◈◈

Mr Collins had come to Longbourn for one reason; Lady Catherine de Bourgh wanted Mr Collins to find a wife. He had a good house near Rosings Park and he had enough money to get married. He knew that the Longbourn estate would belong to* him one day. He thought that it was a good idea to marry one of the Bennet daughters. He didn't change his mind when he met them. He decided to marry Jane Bennet. The next morning, however, he had a short conversation with Mrs Bennet. She explained about Jane and Mr Bingley. Mr Collins was a little disappointed*, but then Mrs Bennet suggested Elizabeth as a possible future Mrs Collins. He was perfectly happy with this change.

◈◈◈

Later, the Bennet girls decided to go for a walk into Meryton. Mr Collins decided to go with them. He talked about Rosings and Lady Catherine de Bourgh all the way into the village. When they arrived, Kitty and Lydia saw one of the officers they knew. He was talking to a tall, handsome young man. Soon, the officer was introducing the man as Mr George Wickham, a new officer in the militia. The Bennet girls

to belong to to own, to have

disappointed unhappy because something that you wanted didn't happen

were very happy to meet Mr Wickham. As well as being handsome, he was very polite. He was also very good at conversation. They were pleased to meet such a gentleman. While they were talking, Mr Darcy and Mr Bingley came into the street on their horses. They bowed* to the Bennet sisters. Mr Darcy was trying not to look at Elizabeth, when he suddenly saw their new friend Mr Wickham. The two men were obviously very shocked. Mr Darcy was very angry and Mr Wickham was very embarrassed. Mr Bingley didn't seem to see. He asked Jane how she was feeling then he and Mr Darcy rode away. There was obviously something strange between Darcy and Wickham. Elizabeth was very curious.

to bow to bend forward, to show respect

Reading Comprehension

1 Answer the questions true (T) or false (F). Correct the false answers.

		T	F
1	Lydia becomes ill while staying at Netherfield.	☐	☐
2	Elizabeth goes to Meryton to see her sister.	☐	☐
3	Elizabeth's dress is muddy when she arrives at Netherfield.	☐	☐
4	In the evening, Elizabeth plays the piano while everyone is playing cards.	☐	☐
5	Mrs Bennet goes to visit Jane and is very polite to Mr Darcy.	☐	☐
6	Caroline Bingley and her sister are unkind about the Bennet family.	☐	☐
7	Mr Bennet isn't happy to see his daughters home.	☐	☐
8	Mr Bingley is coming to stay at Longbourn.	☐	☐
9	Mr Collins arrives for breakfast.	☐	☐
10	Mr Wickham and Mr Darcy are pleased to see each other.	☐	☐

2 Match the pictures to the events in the story.

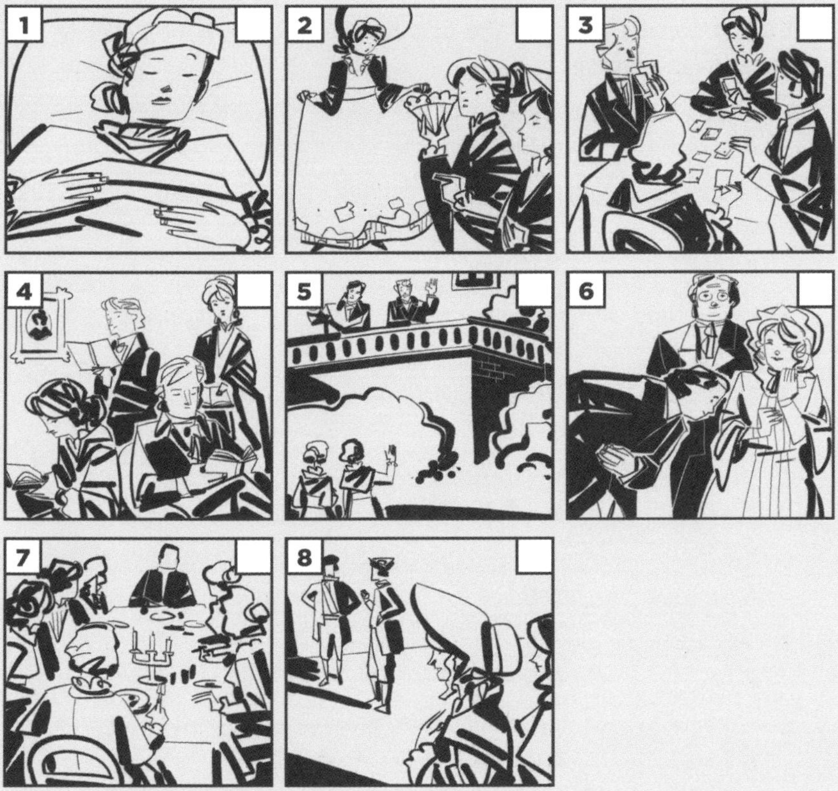

a Mr Collins arrived.

b If everyone was reading a book, Miss Bingley watched Mr Darcy instead of reading her own.

c *'My dearest Lizzy,*
I don't feel very well this morning ...'

d Kitty and Lydia saw one of the officers they knew. He was talking to a tall, handsome young man.

e Mr Bingley's sisters didn't like the fact that Elizabeth's dress was muddy.

f After a few days, Jane was feeling much better and the girls decided to go home.

g After dinner, Elizabeth joined them in the dining room. Everyone was playing cards.

h All through dinner, Mr Collins talked about Lady Catherine de Bourgh.

Grammar

3 Exam Practice. Choose the correct answer – A, B or C. Write the letter in the space.

1 Elizabeth decided to ______ her sister at Netherfield.
A listen **B** visited **C** visit

2 Mr Bingley suggested that Elizabeth should stay ______ Jane was better.
A why **B** which **C** until

3 Mr Bingley says that all young ladies ______ very clever.
A was **B** have **C** are

4 Elizabeth ______ embarrassed by her mother.
A was **B** has **C** are

5 Miss Bingley ______ to mend Mr Darcy's pen.
A asking **B** offered **C** can

6 After a ______ days, Jane was feeling much better.
A several **B** few **C** many

7 Mr Collins arrived ______ four o'clock.
A to **B** in **C** at

8 Mr Bennet and Jane ______ listening to Mr Collins.
A had **B** could **C** enjoyed

9 The Bennet girls were happy ______ Mr Wickham.
A to meet **B** to speak **C** dancing

10 Mr Darcy and Mr Bingley ______ away.
A had **B** arrived **C** rode

4 Reported Speech. Complete the second sentence so it means the same as the first.

1 'I'm much cleverer than Elizabeth.'
Miss Bingley thought she ....

2 'Do you still admire Elizabeth's fine eyes?'
Miss Bingley asked if Mr Darcy ....

3 'All young ladies are so clever,' said Mr Bingley.
Mr Bingley said that ....

4 'I don't know Mr Collins,' said Mr Bennet.
Mr Bennet said that ....

5 'Rosings is one of the finest estates in England,' said Mr Collins.
Mr Collins said that ....

6 'I have many faults,' said Mr Darcy.
Mr Darcy said that ....

PET – Writing

5 You are Mr Collins. You are planning to visit your cousin Mr Bennet.
Write a note to send to Mr Bennet. In your note you should

- say what time you are arriving
- say what day you are arriving
- say how you feel about meeting Mr Bennet

Write 35-45 words

PRE-READING ACTIVITY

Speaking

6 Work in pairs. Discuss.

a In the next chapter, someone wants to marry Elizabeth. Who do you think it is?

- Mr Wickham
- Mr Bingley
- Mr Darcy
- Mr Collins

b What does Elizabeth do? Does she agree to marry the man, or not? Why?

Chapter Three

Mr Wickham's Story

▶ 5 The following evening, the Bennet sisters were invited to a small party at their Aunt Phillips's house in Meryton. Mr Collins was also invited. When they arrived, they were happy to hear that some of the officers were invited, including their new friend, Mr Wickham.

Mr Collins spent the evening comparing Aunt Phillips's house with Rosings Park and telling everyone how much Lady Catherine had spent on a fireplace in her sitting room. All the women in the room were admiring Mr Wickham, including Elizabeth. She was delighted when Mr Wickham came over to talk to her. 'How long has Mr Darcy been here?' Mr Wickham soon asked.

'About a month,' replied Elizabeth, 'I believe he has a large estate in the north of England.'

'Yes, I've known him since I was a child.'

Elizabeth looked surprised.

'You're surprised,' continued Mr Wickham, 'Our meeting yesterday was very cold. What about you, do you know him very well?'

'Not at all,' replied Elizabeth, 'I spent a few days in the same house as him. He's very proud. Nobody here likes him.'

'Is he staying here long?'

'I don't know, but I hope that won't make *you* change *your* plans,' she said firmly*.

firmly in a determined way

'Certainly not,' replied Wickham, 'If he wants to avoid me, he must leave. We are not friends. Mr Darcy's father was a very great man and a true friend. He was very kind to me. His son has not been a true friend. In fact, he has treated me very badly.'*

Elizabeth was very interested in the story, but she was too polite to ask too many questions. Their conversation continued, but they talked about more general things. Elizabeth liked Mr Wickham very much. She asked him why he had joined* the militia.

'I didn't expect to join the militia,' he replied, 'I wanted to join the church. Old Mr Darcy promised me a church on his estate. He was like a father to me and he loved me very much. When old Mr Darcy died, his son gave the church to another man. Now I need a job, so I've joined the militia.'

Elizabeth was very shocked. 'You must tell everyone!' she exclaimed. 'Everyone must know what Mr Darcy is really like.'

'No,' replied Mr Wickham, 'I loved old Mr Darcy like a father. I don't want to bring dishonour* on the Darcy family.'

Elizabeth liked Mr Wickham even more. And she thought he was very handsome indeed. 'Mr Darcy has a sister, I believe.'

'Yes,' answered Mr Wickham, 'she loved me when she was a child, but now she's very proud. She's as proud as her brother.'

A little later, Mr Collins was talking loudly about Lady Catherine de Bourgh and Rosings Park. Mr Wickham spoke quietly to Elizabeth. 'Does Mr Collins know Lady Catherine well?'

'Yes,' replied Elizabeth, 'She is his patron.'

'Lady Catherine is Mr Darcy's aunt. Lady Catherine's daughter will have a lot of money one day. I believe Lady Catherine's daughter is going to marry Mr Darcy.'

to treat someone badly to behave badly to someone
to join to become a part of a group
to bring dishonour to give a bad impression of

Elizabeth was delighted at the news. 'Poor Caroline Bingley,' she thought.

Later that evening, Jane and Elizabeth were talking about the party. Elizabeth explained about Mr Wickham and Mr Darcy. They agreed that it was a terrible thing, but they were both surprised that Mr Bingley liked Mr Darcy so much, when he was such a proud, arrogant man. 'Perhaps it's all a misunderstanding*,' said Jane. Elizabeth laughed. Jane always wanted everyone to be friends.

◈◈◈

A few days later, Mr Bingley and his sisters came to visit the Bennet sisters. Mr Bingley invited them all to a ball at Netherfield the following Tuesday. Mr Collins was invited and the militia officers also had an invitation. Mr Collins surprised Elizabeth later by asking her to dance the first two dances at the ball with him. She had no choice, she had to accept. She was very angry at the situation, because she wanted to dance the first two dances with Mr Wickham. The Bennet girls were excited about the ball, especially Kitty and Lydia. They were so excited that the days until Tuesday seemed to pass very slowly. Everyone agreed that Friday, Saturday, Sunday and Monday were the longest days of their lives.

◈◈◈

On the Tuesday evening, Elizabeth walked into the ballroom at Netherfield and looked around the room. She was looking for Mr Wickham in his red coat. Another officer told her that Wickham had gone to London on business. 'But I don't think he wanted to meet Darcy again,' the officer added.

Elizabeth talked to her friend, Charlotte Lucas, and then it was time

a misunderstanding a mistake

for her two dances with Mr Collins. He was a very bad dancer. Later she danced with another officer. Then, when she was talking to Charlotte again, Mr Darcy came up to her. He asked Elizabeth to dance. Elizabeth was so surprised that she said yes. While they were dancing, they talked a little, but Elizabeth felt very uncomfortable. She was very angry about Mr Wickham. 'When you met us the other day, we were making a new friend.'

'Mr Wickham is very good at *making* friends,' said Mr Darcy angrily, 'but he's not very good at *keeping* them.'

'He's certainly lost your friendship. This has caused him a lot of problems.'

Mr Darcy did not reply. He looked angry. At that moment, Sir William Lucas spoke to Elizabeth. 'This is a fine occasion,' he said, 'We'll have balls like this every week when your sister marries Mr Bingley!'

They continued dancing, but Mr Darcy looked shocked at the idea that his friend was to marry Jane Bennet. He obviously had no idea that people had been talking about Mr Bingley and Jane. Elizabeth was surprised that people were talking about a future marriage, when Mr Bingley and Jane were not engaged*. After a long silence, Mr Darcy suggested they talk about books, but Elizabeth wanted to talk more about Mr Wickham. 'You told me that you have a bad temper. You said that if you have a bad opinion of someone, you never change it.'

'That's true,' replied Mr Darcy.

'Are you always fair* when you decide about a person?'

'Yes, I am.'

'Do you act from pride or prejudice?'

'No, I don't. Why do you ask?'

to be engaged promised to be married to someone

fair right and correct

'I hear different opinions about you from different people,' replied Elizabeth, 'I'm trying to understand your personality.'

At that moment, the dance finished and Elizabeth and Mr Darcy bowed to each other politely, but very coldly. As Elizabeth was walking away, Caroline Bingley came up to talk to her. 'I believe your new favourite is Mr George Wickham,' she said, 'Your youngest sister has been talking to me, she's been asking me thousands of questions about him. Be careful, he's a bad man. He treated poor Mr Darcy in a terrible way. Do you know who he is? He's not a gentleman, he's the son of old Mr Darcy's estate manager.'

'I know that. He told me himself,' replied Elizabeth angrily.

Caroline Bingley laughed unpleasantly* and walked away.

The ball was becoming a nightmare* for Elizabeth. Mr Collins added to her embarrassment when he discovered that Mr Darcy was Lady Catherine de Bourgh's nephew. Mr Collins went immediately to talk to Mr Darcy about Lady Catherine and Rosings. This was a very rude thing to do, as Mr Collins had not met Mr Darcy before. Nobody had introduced them. Mrs Bennet was also behaving very badly. She was talking loudly about Mr Bingley and Jane, 'I'm sure he's going to marry her. Then all my daughters will get rich husbands.'

Everyone could hear. Mr Darcy looked shocked. Elizabeth tried to make her mother shut up.

After dinner, the evening got worse. Mary insisted on singing. She had a terrible voice. She finished the first song and then started a second. Caroline Bingley and her sister were laughing at poor Mary. Eventually, Mr Bennet took her away from the piano. Mr Collins was still talking loudly about Lady Catherine and Rosings Park. He was also making sure that Elizabeth couldn't dance with anyone else.

unpleasantly in a horrible way

a nightmare a bad dream

Kitty and Lydia were dancing happily with all the officers. Elizabeth wanted the evening to end, but the Bennet family and Mr Collins were the last to leave the ball. Mrs Bennet was delighted. She was sure that Mr Bingley and Jane were going to get married. She was also sure that Elizabeth and Mr Collins were going to get married.

◈◈◈

The following morning, Mr Collins asked to speak to Elizabeth alone. This could only mean one thing, he wanted to marry Elizabeth. Mrs Bennet agreed and before Elizabeth could say anything, Mrs Bennet left the room saying, 'Girls, come with me. Lizzy, you stay here and listen to Mr Collins.'

'My dear Miss Elizabeth,' began Mr Collins, '*almost* as soon as I saw you, I decided to marry you. There are three reasons for this. Firstly, I think all clergymen should marry. Secondly, I think marriage will make me happy and thirdly, Lady Catherine de Bourgh thinks it's a good idea. She will visit my future wife very often. This will be such an honour for my future wife. As you know, I will eventually inherit Longbourn. It seems to me that a marriage between you and me would be a very good thing for all your sisters.'

'No!' cried Elizabeth, 'Please stop. I can't marry you.'

Mr Collins smiled. 'I understand,' he said, 'It's quite natural. You're worried about Lady Catherine. Don't worry, my dear Miss Elizabeth. She's a very great lady, but she's very kind to people of lower social status.'

'Mr Collins,' replied Elizabeth, 'you don't understand. You would never be happy with me. I would never be happy with you.'

'Miss Elizabeth. I have a nice house and a good income*. I know you want to marry me. I think you're saying no because that is the fashionable thing to do.'

an income money that you get from working

'No, Mr Collins. I do *not* want to marry you. I will *not* marry you.'

'I will speak to your parents,' said Mr Collins angrily, as Elizabeth left the room.

Mrs Bennet saw Elizabeth leave. She went into the room to speak to Mr Collins. 'Congratulations to you both,' she said.

Then Mr Collins explained the situation. Mrs Bennet was very angry with Elizabeth. 'My husband will speak to her!' she cried.

Mrs Bennet ran into her husband's study. 'Mr Bennet!' she shouted, 'Lizzy will not marry Mr Collins. You must make her marry him. I will never speak to her again if she does not marry Mr Collins.'

'Call Lizzy, my dear,' said Mr Bennet calmly, 'I'll speak to her.'

After a few minutes, Lizzy came into the room. 'Mrs Bennet tells me you will not marry Mr Collins,' said Mr Bennet.

'No, I will not!' said Elizabeth.

'Mmm,' he replied. 'You have a choice. If you don't marry Mr Collins, your mother will never speak to you again,' Mrs Bennet looked very happy. 'But,' continued her husband, 'if you do marry Mr Collins, *I* will never speak to you again.'

'Oh, Mr Bennet!' shouted his wife. She was very angry. 'Now Lizzy will never get married.'

Mr Collins was also very angry. He couldn't understand why Lizzy didn't want to marry him. He thought he was the perfect man. He had a beautiful house, he had a good income but, more importantly, his patron was Lady Catherine de Bourgh. Fortunately, Charlotte Lucas came to visit Elizabeth at that moment. Unlike Elizabeth, she was very happy to talk to Mr Collins. Charlotte and Mr Collins talked for a long time.

Reading Comprehension

1 Match the questions to the answers.

1 ☐ Who were all the women admiring at Aunt Phillips's party?
2 ☐ How does Elizabeth describe Mr Darcy?
3 ☐ What was Mr Collins talking loudly about?
4 ☐ Why wasn't Mr Wickham at the ball?
5 ☐ When Mr Darcy asked Elizabeth to dance, what was her reaction?
6 ☐ How did Elizabeth feel about the Netherfield ball?
7 ☐ What did Mr Collins ask Elizabeth?

a Mr Wickham.
b He asked her to marry him.
c She says he's very proud.
d Lady Catherine de Bourgh and Rosings Park.
e She was so surprised that she said yes.
f He had gone to London.
g It was like a bad dream.

2 Choose the correct answer – A, B or C.

1 Where is Mr Darcy's large estate?
A in the south of England ☐
B in the north of England ☐
C in France ☐

2 How long has Mr Wickham known Mr Darcy?
A for a few weeks ☐
B since he came to Meryton ☐
C since he was a child ☐

3 Are Mr Wickham and Mr Darcy friends?
A yes ☐
B we don't know ☐
C no ☐

4 Does Elizabeth like Mr Wickham?
A yes ☐
B we don't know ☐
C no ☐

5 What relation is Lady Catherine de Bourgh to Mr Darcy?

A she's his mother ☐
B she's his sister ☐
C she's his aunt ☐

6 What does Caroline Bingley say about Mr Wickham?

A that he's a bad man ☒
B that he's a handsome man ☐
C that he's an interesting man ☐

7 What does Elizabeth say when Mr Collins proposes to her?

A 'I will not marry you.' ☒
B 'I will marry you.' ☐
C 'Why don't you marry Jane?' ☐

Grammar

so + adjective or adverb *he was **so rich**, she played the piano **so well**.*
such + noun *he was **such** a rich **man.***

3 So and Such. Complete the sentences with *so* or *such*.

1 Mr Darcy was ______ proud that no-one liked him.
2 Elizabeth was ______ surprised that she said yes.
3 Lady Catherine de Bourgh was ______ a great lady.
4 Mr Darcy was ______ an arrogant man.
5 They were ______ excited that the days seemed to pass very slowly.
6 It will be ______ an honour for my future wife.

4 First Conditional. Match the beginnings and the endings of these sentences.

1 ☐ If you don't marry Mr Collins,
2 ☐ If you marry Mr Collins,
3 ☐ If Mr Darcy asks me to dance,
4 ☐ If Mr Bingley marries Jane,
5 ☐ If Mr Collins gets married,
6 ☐ If Elizabeth marries Mr Collins,

a there will be balls at Netherfield all the time.
b Lady Catherine de Bourgh will visit his new wife.
c she'll be very unhappy.
d I will never speak to you again.
e your mother will never speak to you again.
f I'll say no.

Writing

5 **Write about Mr Wickham. Think about his physical description, his character and his life. Use the words in the box to help you. You can use your own ideas too.**

handsome • a red coat • Mr Darcy • a soldier • good at conversation
friendly • poor • a gentleman • old Mr Darcy • tall

PET – Reading

6 **Look at the description of these books and magazines. Choose one for each of these characters to read.**

1 Mr Darcy is an educated gentleman. He is quite shy and reserved. He has a large country estate in Derbyshire. He spends some time in London. He enjoys reading and is interested in politics and he also likes philosophy and history.

2 Miss Mary Bennet is very fond of music, although she isn't very good at playing the piano. She also likes reading very serious books. She is very interested in religious affairs. She prefers staying at home to going out to parties and balls.

3 Mr Bingley doesn't like reading very much. He likes riding and is generally interested in sport and country life. He's also quite interested in people. He's intelligent, but he doesn't like reading serious books.

4 Miss Charlotte Lucas quite likes reading. She is a quiet, serious girl. She isn't very romantic and she isn't interested in fashion. She really wants to get married, so she can have a house of her own. She is interested in cooking and in home décor.

The Fashionable Lady
All the latest fashions from Paris. This review contains advice for ladies about dress styles for family parties and formal balls as well as country weekends.

The Book of Household Management
This excellent handbook contains everything you need to know about the home. It contains recipes and general kitchen advice, information about home style and some designs for gardens.

Country Life
This is the most popular magazine for country gentlemen. It has articles about everything concerning life in the country, but its main focus is horses and horse-riding. The style of writing is practical and interesting.

The Magazine for Ladies
This is an excellent new magazine for serious young ladies. It has articles about everything an educated young lady should know, such as drawing, music and languages.

The History of England
This three-monthly review has articles about the history of England. This issue focuses on events in the reign of Queen Elizabeth I. This publication is highly recommended for serious, educated people.

The Gentleman's Magazine
This popular magazine is now in its twentieth year. It's a general review with articles about politics, country issues and philosophy. This month's issue has an in-depth report about the implications of the French Revolution.

Regency Furniture
Everything the country gentleman needs to know about taste and design in furniture. This month's magazine has information about chairs for country houses and contains a directory of fashionable London furniture-makers.

PRE-READING ACTIVITY

PET – Speaking

7 a Work in pairs. Each of you is going to talk on your own for about a minute.

Student A turn to page 41.
Look at the picture. Tell your partner what you can see.
Student B turn to page 51.
Look at the picture. Tell your partner what you can see.

7 b What do you think is going to happen in the next chapter?

Chapter Four

Jane Goes to London

▶ 6 The following morning, the younger Bennet girls decided to walk to Meryton. Elizabeth was happy to go with them because Mrs Bennet was still angry with her. They met Mr Wickham in Meryton and they all went to see Aunt Phillips. As usual, Aunt Phillips was happy to see her young visitors. They chatted and drank tea and Mr Wickham soon explained to Elizabeth why he hadn't gone to the ball. 'I didn't want to embarrass Mr Bingley and I didn't want to be in the same room as Mr Darcy, either.'

Elizabeth liked Mr Wickham's answer.

◈◈◈

Just after they arrived home, a letter came for Jane from Caroline Bingley. Jane read the letter. She looked sad. 'Everyone has left Netherfield. They've gone to London and they're not going to come back. Caroline has asked me to write to her.'

'Maybe they'll come back for Christmas,' said Elizabeth.

'No, listen,' said Jane, as she read from the letter.

'...many of our friends are in London. Mr Darcy wants to see his sister. My brother also wants to see her. Miss Darcy is very beautiful and my brother likes her very much. I really hope that they will get married one day. We will all be so happy if they do.'

'So,' said Jane sadly, 'Mr Bingley doesn't love me. Caroline is very kind, she wants me to know.'

Jane was kind-hearted* and she always thought the best of people. Elizabeth was more realistic. 'I don't think so!' cried Elizabeth, 'Charles Bingley loves you, I'm sure. You love him. Miss Bingley wants her brother to marry Miss Darcy and she wants to marry Mr Darcy herself. They have taken Mr Bingley away. They want to keep him in London to separate you. Our family isn't rich or important enough for them.'

◆◆◆

Mr Collins was still staying at Longbourn and Mrs Bennet now hoped that he would marry Mary, or one of the other girls. However, Mr Collins had a different plan. He was spending a lot of time with Charlotte Lucas and her family. Charlotte and her family were delighted when Mr Collins asked her to marry him. It was a very good marriage for Charlotte. She was twenty-seven years old and most girls her age were already married. Mr Collins had a good house and good connections*. The one problem was Mr Collins himself; he was irritating and not really a very nice man. Fortunately, Charlotte wasn't very romantic.

They kept the engagement secret until Mr Collins had left Longbourn. After he had gone back to tell Lady Catherine his exciting news, Charlotte went to tell Elizabeth. Elizabeth was horrified*. She thought her friend was making a terrible mistake. 'Engaged to Mr Collins? Impossible!' cried Elizabeth.

'Why are you surprised?' replied Charlotte calmly. 'You didn't want to marry him. I do. I'm not romantic, you know. I have never been romantic. I just need a comfortable home and Mr Collins can give me that.'

kind-hearted kind and generous
connections social relationships
horrified shocked

When Mrs Bennet heard the news, she was very upset*. She didn't say a kind word to Elizabeth for a week and she was rude to Lady Lucas for the next month. Lady Lucas didn't help; she visited Longbourn more often than usual to talk about her happiness.

◈◈◈

Jane had replied to Caroline Bingley's letter very quickly. She was waiting for her friend to write again. Two or three weeks later, a second letter from Caroline arrived. The letter confirmed that Mr Bingley didn't want to come back to Netherfield. He was staying with Mr Darcy in London. Caroline's letter was full of information about Miss Darcy and how beautiful she was. Jane was now sure that Mr Bingley didn't love her. She was very unhappy.

Fortunately, Mr Wickham visited Longbourn frequently. He was good company and very popular in the village. Everyone now knew the story about Mr Darcy and Mr Wickham. Everyone agreed that Mr Wickham was a true gentleman and that Mr Darcy was a very bad man.

◈◈◈

Mrs Bennet's brother, Mr Gardiner, and his wife came to spend Christmas at Longbourn. They lived in London and often came to visit Longbourn with their children. The Bennet sisters were always very happy when their London relatives came to stay. Mrs Gardiner could tell them all about the latest fashions and she always brought lots of presents for them. Elizabeth was fond of her Uncle and Aunt Gardiner, so she often wrote to them. Mrs Gardiner knew the whole story about Jane and Mr Bingley and she was sad for Jane. 'Jane, you must come to London with us after Christmas,' she said one evening, 'The change will be good for you.'

upset angry (also means sad)

Jane was very happy with the plan. The Gardiners didn't live in a fashionable area of London and they didn't go to fashionable parties. As a result, Jane didn't expect to see Mr Bingley while she was in London, but she expected Caroline Bingley to visit her. Caroline was her friend.

◇◇◇

The Gardiners stayed at Longbourn for a week. The Christmas celebrations were very enjoyable. The Gardiners and the Bennets went to parties every night and they often met Mr Wickham. Mrs Gardiner often talked to Mr Wickham, because she came from the same area of the country, Derbyshire. They talked about Derbyshire, Pemberley and the Darcy family. Mr Wickham told her all about his problems with Mr Darcy and Mrs Gardiner was convinced that Mr Darcy was the proudest, most unpleasant man in England. Mrs Gardiner was worried, however, she didn't want Elizabeth to fall in love with Mr Wickham. One evening, she talked to Elizabeth about him. 'Mr Wickham is a very fine man,' said Mrs Gardiner, 'but you can't marry him, you know. He has no money.'

'I know. Don't worry, Aunt,' said Elizabeth smiling, 'I'm not in love with Mr Wickham and he's not in love with me!'

◇◇◇

After Christmas, Jane went to London with the Gardiners. Elizabeth missed her very much. Charlotte Lucas was busy with her wedding preparations, so Elizabeth had time to write long letters to Jane. Mr Collins soon came back from his short trip home to tell Lady Catherine that he was engaged. This time, he stayed at the Lucas's family home.

◇◇◇

The day before she got married, Charlotte visited Elizabeth. 'You must write to me often,' said Charlotte.

'Of course I will,' replied Elizabeth.

'And I have a favour* to ask. I'm going to miss Meryton and all my friends here when I move to Mr Collins's house in Hunsford. In March, my father and my sister are coming to stay with me in Hunsford. Will you come with them too?'

'Of course!' said Elizabeth. She had no choice. She had to accept the invitation, although she didn't really want to go and stay with Mr Collins and his new wife.

Charlotte and Mr Collins got married and moved to Hunsford. Elizabeth missed her friend very much.

◈◈◈

A letter soon arrived from Jane. She had been in London for a week, and had not seen Caroline Bingley. Jane was a little surprised, because she had written to Caroline and Caroline hadn't answered her letter.

> *'I'm going to visit Caroline Bingley tomorrow,'* wrote Jane, *'I'm sure she didn't get my letter.'*

A few days later, Elizabeth received another letter from Jane.

> *'I went to see Caroline yesterday. She was very happy to see me. She hadn't received my letter. I asked about Mr Bingley. Caroline said he was very busy with Mr Darcy. Caroline said that Miss Darcy was coming to dinner that evening. My visit was very short, because Caroline and her sister were going out. I'm sure Caroline will come to visit me soon.'*

a favour some help

Elizabeth was not so sure and, this time, Elizabeth was right. Jane waited at home every day for two weeks, but Caroline didn't visit. Finally, after a month, Caroline Bingley came. Jane's next letter to Elizabeth was very sad.

'...she finally came to visit. She obviously didn't want to come. She was rude to me. She stayed for a very short time and when she left, she didn't say she wanted to see me again. She's worried about Mr Bingley, she doesn't want him to marry me. She talked about Miss Darcy all the time. She really isn't my friend. I'm very unhappy, but Mr and Mrs Gardiner are very kind to me. Have a good time in Hunsford and give my love to Charlotte.'

Elizabeth was sad for Jane, but she was happy about one thing: Jane now understood that Caroline was not a true friend.

◈◈◈

Elizabeth had some news from Meryton to give to Mrs Gardiner in her next letter to her aunt. Mr Wickham was getting married. He was getting married to a Miss King. Unlike Elizabeth, Miss King was very rich. Elizabeth told her aunt that she was not unhappy, but Kitty and Lydia were very sad. Elizabeth thought that Mr Wickham had no choice, because he needed to marry a rich woman. Charlotte had married Mr Collins for a comfortable life, and now Mr Wickham was marrying for money. Elizabeth still thought Charlotte had made a mistake, but she was much kinder to Mr Wickham than she was to Charlotte.

◈◈◈

Life in the country went on as normal and soon March arrived. Elizabeth started to get ready for her trip to Hunsford. She planned to travel with Sir William Lucas and Charlotte's sister Maria. They decided to stay for one night in London with Mr and Mrs Gardiner and then to continue to Hunsford the following day. Elizabeth was very happy to see Jane again. Mrs Gardiner also had an invitation for Elizabeth. She and her husband were planning to visit the north of England in the summer. They wanted to visit Derbyshire and they wanted Elizabeth to go with them. She was delighted.

Reading Comprehension

1 Choose the best answer – A, B or C. Write the letter in the space.

1 ______ sent a letter to Jane to say everyone had gone to London.
A Elizabeth **B** Caroline Bingley **C** Mr Darcy

2 Mr Collins asked ______ to marry him.
A Mary Bennet **B** Charlotte Lucas **C** Jane Bennet

3 Jane was sure that Mr Bingley ______ her.
A loved **B** didn't love **C** wanted to marry

4 Elizabeth's ______ came to Longbourn for Christmas.
A niece and nephew **B** mother and father **C** aunt and uncle

5 Mrs Gardiner comes from the same area of England as ______.
A Mr Wickham **B** Mr Collins **C** Mr Bingley

6 Mrs Gardiner didn't want Elizabeth to ______ Mr Wickham.
A speak to **B** fall in love with **C** hold hands with

7 After Christmas Jane ______.
A went to London **B** became ill **C** visited Mr Collins

8 Caroline Bingley ______ Jane for a long time.
A invited **B** cried about **C** didn't visit

9 Jane wrote to Elizabeth and told her she was ______.
A very sad **B** very ill **C** very tired

10 Mr and Mrs Gardiner invited ______ to go to Derbyshire with them in the summer.
A Mr Collins **B** Elizabeth **C** Mrs Bennet

2 Put the following events in the correct order.

a Elizabeth starts to get ready for her trip to Hunsford.
b Jane goes to London.
c Elizabeth is shocked at Charlotte's engagement.
d Mr and Mrs Gardiner come for Christmas.
e Charlotte asks Elizabeth to visit her in Hunsford.
f Mr Wickham explains why he wasn't at the Netherfield ball.
g Elizabeth hears news that Mr Wickham is going to get married for money.
h Caroline Bingley visits Jane in London.
i Jane gets a letter saying everyone has gone to London.

f								

Grammar

3 Past Simple: affirmative and negative. Complete the sentences using the past simple of the verb in brackets.

1 Aunt Phillips ________ happy to see her young visitors. (be)
2 I ________ to embarrass Mr Bingley. (not want)
3 A letter ________ for Jane from Caroline Bingley. (come)
4 They ________ the engagement secret. (keep)
5 She ________ a kind word to Elizabeth for a week. (not say)
6 Mr Wickham ________ Longbourn frequently. (visit)
7 Everyone ________ that Mr Wickham ________ a true gentleman. (agree; be)
8 Mrs Gardiner ________ the whole story about Jane and Mr Bingley. (know)
9 Elizabeth ________ Jane very much. (miss)
10 Jane ________ at home every day for two weeks. (wait)

4 Past Simple: questions. Put the questions into the correct order. Then match the questions with the answers.

1 Mr Wickham/Why/go to the ball/didn't
2 go/Where/the younger Bennet girls/did
3 Charlotte Lucas/was/How old
4 horrified/Elizabeth/was/Why
5 When/arrive/the letter/did/from Caroline Bingley
6 a fashionable area of London/Did/live/the Gardiners/in
7 London/When/Jane/did/go to
8 Caroline Bingley/How long/stay/did
9 propose to/Who/Mr Wickham/did
10 Elizabeth/before she went to Hunsford/did/Where/stay

1 ☐ ______________________?
2 ☐ ______________________?
3 ☐ ______________________?
4 ☐ ______________________?
5 ☐ ______________________?
6 ☐ ______________________?
7 ☐ ______________________?
8 ☐ ______________________?
9 ☐ ______________________?
10 ☐ ______________________?

a A few weeks later.
b For a very short time.
c After Christmas.
d Because Charlotte wanted to marry Mr Collins.
e Miss King.
f London.
g Meryton.
h Twenty-seven.
i He didn't want to embarrass Mr Bingley.
j No, they didn't.

PET – Writing

5 You are Mrs Collins. You want to invite your friend Elizabeth to visit you at Hunsford. Write the invitation you send to Elizabeth. You should

- invite Elizabeth
- tell her when to come
- say what you can do together when she arrives

Write 35-45 words

PET - Listening

▶ 7 **6 Listen to the beginning of the next chapter and answer the questions, true (T) or false (F).**

	T	F
1 Elizabeth was very excited on the journey.	☐	☐
2 Charlotte was unhappy to see her friend.	☐	☐
3 Mr Bingley showed them around the house.	☐	☐
4 Elizabeth thought Mr Collins was trying to make her feel good.	☐	☐
5 Mr Collins wasn't very busy.	☐	☐
6 Mr Collins talked a lot about Lady Catherine de Bourgh.	☐	☐
7 Elizabeth wasn't very curious about Lady Catherine.	☐	☐
8 Elizabeth was very curious about Lady Catherine's daughter.	☐	☐
9 Anne de Bourgh was going to marry Mr Bingley.	☐	☐
10 An invitation to dinner never came.	☐	☐

Speaking

7 Work in pairs. In the next chapter, Elizabeth meets Lady Catherine de Bourgh, Mr Collins's patron. What do you think Lady Catherine is like? Think about the following

- house
- money
- character
- manners

Chapter Five

Lady Catherine de Bourgh

7 Elizabeth loved travelling, so she was very excited on the journey to see Charlotte. When they arrived in Hunsford, Charlotte was delighted to see her friend. Mr Collins was also waiting for them. He showed them around the house. Elizabeth felt that Mr Collins was trying to make her feel bad. After all, he had asked Elizabeth to marry him first. Mrs Collins seemed happy with her life, especially because her husband was very busy and was often out or in his study. Of course, Mr Collins talked a lot about Lady Catherine de Bourgh and Rosings Park, her fine estate. Elizabeth was beginning to feel very curious about the lady. Elizabeth was also very curious about Lady Catherine's daughter, Miss Anne de Bourgh. Anne, of course, was going to marry Mr Darcy, if Caroline Bingley didn't marry him first. Fortunately, after a few days, an invitation to dinner at Rosings Park came.

8 Mr Collins spent a long time giving orders to Maria Lucas, Charlotte's sister, about the dinner. He told her what clothes to wear and how to do her hair. Sir William Lucas was very nervous about meeting the great Lady Catherine. Elizabeth was looking forward to* the dinner. As they walked up to Rosings, a very fine house, Mr Collins told them

to look forward to to be excited about something which is going to happen

how many windows there were and how much they had cost. They were introduced to Lady Catherine and to her daughter. Elizabeth was pleased to see that Mr Darcy's future wife was quiet, pale and looked quite ill. The dinner was very good and there were lots of servants, but Lady Catherine talked all the time in a loud voice. She had an opinion about everything. Sir William was still very nervous and said very little. Maria was totally silent. Mr Collins agreed with everything Lady Catherine said. Finally, Lady Catherine spoke to Elizabeth, who was not at all nervous. 'Do you play and sing, Miss Bennet?' she asked.

'A little,' replied Elizabeth.

'One day, you must come and play here.'

Lady Catherine continued to ask questions. She often interrupted people's answers and Elizabeth thought she was very rude. 'Miss Bennet, are all your sisters out*? Do they all go to balls and dances?'

'Yes, all my sisters are out,' she replied politely.

'That is not a good thing. Younger sisters should stay at home. They must not go to balls and parties until the older sisters are married.'

'Oh, I think that would be very unfair,' said Elizabeth.

Everyone was shocked, especially Mr Collins. Elizabeth had disagreed with Lady Catherine de Bourgh. 'Hmmm,' said Lady Catherine. She thought Elizabeth was very impertinent*.

◈◈◈

After a week, Sir William went home, leaving Elizabeth and Maria to stay with Charlotte. Mr Collins walked to Rosings almost every day. Sometimes Lady Catherine visited them. When she came, she gave a lot of orders. About twice a week, they had dinner at Rosings. One evening, Lady Catherine told them that she had visitors for Easter.

out introduced to people in society. Able to go to parties and balls
impertinent rude (to an older person)

The visitors were Mr Darcy and his cousin Colonel Fitzwilliam. Lady Catherine obviously liked Mr Darcy very much. The colonel and Mr Darcy soon came to visit Mrs Collins. Colonel Fitzwilliam was very polite. Mr Darcy was very quiet. He spent most of the visit looking out of the window. Just before they left, he asked Elizabeth a question. 'How are your mother and father and all your sisters?'

'Very well, thank you,' Elizabeth replied, 'My sister Jane has been in London for the last three months. Have you seen her?'

'No, I haven't,' said Mr Darcy.

Elizabeth thought he was embarrassed.

◈◈◈

A week later, Lady Catherine sent a dinner invitation to Mr and Mrs Collins, Elizabeth and Maria. When they arrived at Rosings, Lady Catherine said very little to them; she just continued speaking to Mr Darcy. Colonel Fitzwilliam and Elizabeth chatted about books and music. After a few minutes, Lady Catherine interrupted their conversation. 'What are you talking about?' she said loudly. Lady Catherine was irritated because she wasn't part of the conversation. 'What are you saying to Miss Bennet?' she said.

'Music, Lady Catherine. We are talking about music,' Colonel Fitzwilliam replied.

'Ah music. Darcy,' said Lady Catherine loudly, 'how is your sister? She is a very good musician.'

'She is very well, thank you, Lady Catherine,' Mr Darcy replied.

Mr Darcy was ashamed of* his aunt's manners, particularly when she continued to dominate the conversation for a long time.

After coffee, Colonel Fitzwilliam asked Elizabeth to play the piano and sing for them. Lady Catherine talked loudly to Mr Darcy for most

ashamed of embarrassed by

of the song, until Mr Darcy walked away to stand near the piano.

Elizabeth continued to play. At the end of the song, she spoke to Mr Darcy. 'I'm not afraid of you,' she said, 'I know your sister plays and sings very well, but you can't make me afraid.'

'I'm not trying to make you, afraid,' he replied, 'You always pretend not to understand people.'

'Now Colonel Fitzwilliam will think I pretend all the time! He'll never believe a word I say,' said Elizabeth smiling. 'I will punish you by telling the colonel about your, terrible behaviour in Meryton.'

'I'm not afraid of you, either,' said Mr Darcy. He was smiling too.

'Tell me about Darcy's behaviour!' said the colonel.

'He behaved very badly at a dance in Meryton. He only danced four times and there were lots of ladies who couldn't dance because they didn't have a partner.'

Mr Darcy tried to explain. 'I didn't know the ladies. They were all strangers. I'm not very good at talking to strangers.'

'I'm not very good at playing the piano,' replied Elizabeth, 'but that's because I don't practise enough!'

'It's a pleasure to listen to you,' said Mr Darcy.

At that moment, Lady Catherine interrupted. 'Miss Bennet needs to practise more,' she said loudly. 'Anne has never learnt to play the piano, but she would play much better.'

Elizabeth was very polite, but she thought Lady Catherine was extremely rude.

◆◆◆

The next morning, Elizabeth was by herself. Charlotte and Maria were in the village, so she decided to write to Jane. There was a ring at the door and a moment later, Mr Darcy walked into the room. He sat down. Elizabeth was surprised. Conversation was very difficult, so Elizabeth asked about Mr Bingley. 'Is Mr Bingley planning to come back to Netherfield?'

'I don't think he'll return,' replied Mr Darcy.

Mr Darcy decided to continue the conversation. 'Mr Collins has made a good choice of wife. And she's lucky to be so near her family.'

'Near?' said Elizabeth, 'She's a long way from home.'

They talked a little more about Longbourn, Rosings and the countryside. Then Mr Darcy left, just as Charlotte and Maria were coming home. 'He must be in love with you!' said Charlotte, 'Why else did he come here?'

'He probably had nothing better to do,' replied Elizabeth, 'Lady Catherine's very boring.'

◈◈◈

In the following days, Darcy visited several times. He said very little and often sat silently. Elizabeth sometimes met him when she was out walking, but he had very little to say. One day, Elizabeth was out walking when she met Colonel Fitzwilliam. He walked with her for a while. They chatted about London and Elizabeth asked if he knew Mr Bingley. 'Yes, he is a great friend of Darcy's,' said the colonel, 'I think Darcy looks after Charles Bingley very well. He helped Bingley very much, recently. Bingley wanted to marry a woman, but Darcy didn't think it was a good marriage. The woman was very pretty, but her family didn't have very good connections. Darcy and Bingley's sisters took him to London.'

Elizabeth was very shocked. Her mind was racing*. She realised that the colonel was talking about Jane. Charles Bingley really was in love

her mind was racing she was thinking very fast

with Jane. He wanted to marry Jane and Mr Darcy had stopped him. That horrible, proud Mr Darcy had separated Mr Bingley and Jane. The next few minutes were very difficult as Elizabeth tried to control her feelings. She and the colonel walked as far as the parsonage*. They said goodbye and Elizabeth ran inside. Charlotte saw Elizabeth's face. She knew something was wrong.

'I have a headache,' said Elizabeth, taking off her hat, 'I can't go to Rosings for tea. You go, I'll stay here.'

Mr Collins, Charlotte and Maria left Elizabeth and walked to Rosings Park.

◈◈◈

Elizabeth was in the sitting room, thinking, when Mr Darcy walked in. She was shocked and she really didn't want to talk to him. It was clear that Mr Darcy had something important to say. 'Miss Bennet,' he began, 'I must tell you. I've tried, but I can't control my feelings. I love you, very much.'

Elizabeth was silent. She didn't know what to say. Mr Darcy carried on talking. He talked about his love for her, but he also talked about his family. He compared his family to her family. He talked about pride and his position in society. He said that her family was inferior to* his. At first, Elizabeth was sorry. She didn't like Mr Darcy, but she didn't want to hurt him. But when he insulted* her family, she began to get angry. She thought about Jane and Mr Bingley. 'Mr Darcy,' she said, 'it's normal to thank a man for his proposal* of marriage. I can't thank you. I don't like you. I can't marry you.'

Mr Darcy was very surprised. He was also very angry. 'Your answer wasn't very polite,' he said. He was trying to be calm.

'Your proposal wasn't very polite,' said Elizabeth. She was trying

a parsonage a clergyman's house
inferior to lower than
to insult to say bad things about someone
a proposal an offer of marriage

to control her feelings too. 'I will never marry you. You've insulted my family and you've made my sister very unhappy.'

'I'm sorry if your sister is unhappy,' said Mr Darcy coldly, 'but I separated my friend from your sister for very good reasons.'

'I have another reason!' Elizabeth was now very angry. 'Mr Wickham told me all about you. You made him poor. You treated him very badly!'

'Is this your opinion of me? You are angry because I am honest. I have told you what I think about your family. Your pride is hurt.'

'You're wrong, Mr Darcy!' Elizabeth replied. 'I've never liked you. You're proud. You're arrogant. I saw this the moment I met you. You don't care about other people. You have not behaved like a gentleman this evening. I could never marry you.'

'You've said enough,' replied Mr Darcy icily*, 'I understand perfectly. I'm sorry. I hope you'll be very happy in the future.' He walked quickly out of the room.

Elizabeth was very confused. She thought about Jane, she thought about Mr Wickham. 'Why did Mr Darcy love her?' she thought, 'He was so very proud.'

icily very coldly

Reading Comprehension

1 Answer the questions, true (T) or false (F). Correct the false answers in your exercise book.

	T	F
1 Elizabeth is curious about Lady Catherine de Bourgh.	☐	☐
2 Lady Catherine de Bourgh is very quiet.	☐	☐
3 Elizabeth thinks that Lady Catherine is very polite.	☐	☐
4 Mr Bingley comes to stay at Rosings Park.	☐	☐
5 Elizabeth discovers Mr Collins has stopped Bingley from marrying Jane.	☐	☐
6 Mr Darcy says that he thinks Elizabeth's family are inferior to his.	☐	☐
7 Elizabeth agrees to marry Mr Darcy.	☐	☐

2 Which characters say these things? You can use the characters more than once. Not all characters are used.

Elizabeth Bennet • Mr Bingley • Mr Collins • Colonel Fitzwilliam
Lady Catherine de Bourgh • Charlotte Collins (Lucas)
Mr Darcy • Mrs Bennet

1 'That is not a good thing. Younger sisters should stay at home. They must not go to balls and parties until the older sisters are married.'
2 'My sister Jane has been in London for the last three months. Have you seen her?'
3 'Music, Lady Catherine. We are talking about music.'
4 'How is your sister? She is a very good musician.'
5 'I'm not very good at talking to strangers.'
6 'I'm not very good at playing the piano, but that is because I don't practise enough.'
7 'He must be in love with you. Why else did he come here?'
8 'You have insulted my family and you've made my sister very unhappy.'

Grammar

Adjectives usually give you more information about people and places.
Lady Catherine de Bourgh was a very ***rich*** *lady.*
Adverbs usually give you more information about how things happen.
Lady Catherine spoke ***loudly****.*
Adverbs often end **-ly**

3 Adjectives and Adverbs. Use the adverbs and adjectives in the box to complete the sentences.

curious • quiet • polite • badly • loudly • embarrassed
boring • rudely • well • icily

1 Elizabeth was very *curious* to meet Lady Catherine de Bourgh.
2 Lady Catherine was __________. She talked about herself all the time.
3 It was difficult for other people to have conversations, she talked so __________.
4 Mr Darcy was __________ by his aunt's rude behaviour.
5 Colonel Fitzwilliam talked a lot, but Darcy was very __________.
6 Lady Catherine often interrupted people __________.
7 In contrast to Lady Catherine, Elizabeth was very __________.
8 Elizabeth wanted to play the piano very __________.
9 'You treated Mr Wickham very __________,' cried Elizabeth.
10 'You have said enough,' said Mr Darcy __________.

4 Present Perfect. Complete the sentences using the present perfect of the verb in brackets. Use the short form where possible.

1 My sister Jane ____ ______ in London for the last three months. (be)
2 __________ you _____ her? (see)
3 I ____ ______ Jane. (not see)
4 Anne _____ never __________ to play the piano. (learn)
5 Mr Collins ____ ______ a good choice of wife. (make)
6 You ____ ______ like a gentleman this evening. (not behave)
7 I _____ never __________ you. (like)
8 You ____ ______ enough. (say)

5 Look at the text in each question. What does it say? Choose the correct explanation – A, B or C.

1

ROSINGS PARK
ESTATE PRIVATE
KEEP OUT

A Everyone is welcome to visit. ☐
B No soldiers are allowed on the estate. ☐
C No-one is allowed to enter. ☐

2

Dear Elizabeth,
Come for dinner tonight at 8pm instead of 7.30.
My father's going to be late home.
Your friend,
Charlotte

A Dinner is at 8 pm tonight. ☐
B Charlotte's father is arriving home at 8 pm. ☐
C Charlotte doesn't like dinner at 7.30 pm. ☐

3

Dear Charlotte,
Did I leave some gloves at your house on Thursday? I can't find them anywhere.
It's a bit of a problem because I borrowed them from Jane!
Could you have a look for them?
Your friend,
Elizabeth

A Elizabeth has lost Charlotte's gloves. ☐
B Elizabeth's hands are cold. ☐
C Elizabeth wants Charlotte to look for her gloves. ☐

4

MERYTON BALL
Friday at 8pm at the Assembly Rooms.
Music: The Village People.
PLEASE LET MARY BENNET
KNOW IF YOU CAN'T COME.

A Mary Bennet wants everyone to come to the ball. ☐
B The ball is at Netherfield. ☐
C You should tell Mary Bennet if you can't attend the ball. ☐

PET - Writing

6 This is part of a letter you have received from an English friend. **Write your reply in about 100 words.**

> *My journey to Hunsford was very long, but I love travelling.*
> *In your next letter, please tell me all about a journey you have made.*
> *Why did you enjoy it?*

PRE-READING ACTIVITY

Speaking

7 **Work in pairs. Discuss.**
In the next chapter, Mr Darcy writes Elizabeth a long letter. It contains the phrase
'This is the true story of my family's connection with Mr Wickham.'

What do you think is 'the true story'? Compare your answers with other students.

Chapter Six

Mr Darcy's Letter

9 The following morning, Elizabeth woke up with a terrible headache. She was still very shocked and confused about Mr Darcy's proposal. She decided to go out for a walk in the countryside to clear her head. She walked for a long way and was beginning to feel much better, when suddenly, she saw a man on the road. It was Mr Darcy. He called her name. Elizabeth stopped. Mr Darcy was holding a letter. 'Please read this letter,' he said.

Elizabeth took the letter. Mr Darcy bowed then walked quickly away. Elizabeth opened it.

Dear Miss Bennet,
Do not be afraid, this is not another proposal of marriage. You must read this letter. You are angry about Mr Bingley and your sister. You are also angry about Mr Wickham. I have some things to say about both. First of all, I would like to explain about Mr Bingley.

When I was in Netherfield, I realised that Mr Bingley liked your sister very much. On the evening of the Netherfield ball, I saw that Charles was in love with your sister. While you and I were dancing, Sir William Lucas spoke to us. He said that Charles Bingley and your sister were going to get married. Everyone obviously thought this.
I watched your sister for the rest of the evening. She smiled a lot, she

was open and she was happy, but I saw no evidence that she was in love with Charles. You said yesterday that she was very unhappy. I'm sorry about this. Perhaps I was wrong. Perhaps she was in love with Charles. However, there are other reasons why a marriage between your sister and Charles Bingley would be a bad idea.
Your family status is not very high, although your father is a gentleman. This would not be a problem, if your mother and your younger sisters behaved better. You and your older sister are different. I'm sorry to offend you, but this is true.*
When Charles went to London on business, I decided to follow him. I decided to make him stay in London for the winter. His sisters agreed with me. They didn't want him to marry your sister. We talked to him about your sister. We explained that she was not in love with him. Bingley is a modest man, he trusted our advice. I am not sorry about this, I believe I was right. There is one thing that I am less happy about. I didn't tell Charles that your sister was in London. Perhaps that was a mistake. I knew and his sisters knew, but we decided not to tell him. However, I am not sorry about anything else, I acted for very good reasons.

Secondly, you say that I am the reason that Mr Wickham is poor. I don't want to tell you, but I have no choice. I must tell you the whole story about Mr Wickham and my family.
Mr Wickham is the son of a very good man who was the manager of my family's estate at Pemberley. My father was very fond of George Wickham and he helped him very much. George Wickham's father was very poor, so my father paid for the boy to go to school and then to Cambridge University. My father hoped that George would become a clergyman. I knew that Mr George Wickham was not a good man.

to offend to make someone angry by saying something negative to them or about them

He behaved badly at Cambridge. My father never saw this and I never told him.
Just before my father died, about five years ago, he asked me to give Mr Wickham a church on the Pemberley estate. I agreed.
Six months later, Mr Wickham wrote to me. He said he had no intention of becoming a clergyman. He asked me to give him some money instead of the family church. He intended to study law. I was happy to pay him some money, because I thought Mr Wickham would be a bad clergyman. I paid him three thousand pounds. There was no reason for any more contact between us. I didn't like him. He didn't like me.

Three years later, he wrote to me again. He said he had changed his mind and wanted to become a clergyman after all. He asked me to give him the church on the Pemberley estate. I said no. There was no reason for him to contact me again.

Last summer, however, he did a terrible thing. I don't want to tell anyone this, but I trust you to keep my family's secret. My sister Georgiana was fifteen years old. She left school last year and moved to London. Her housekeeper and companion was called Mrs Younge. Georgiana and Mrs Younge went to the seaside in the summer and Mr Wickham met them there. Mr Wickham paid Georgiana a lot of attention. She thought she was in love with him. She agreed to marry Mr Wickham in secret. She was only fifteen! Fortunately, I went to the seaside to visit them, two days before they planned to run away* together. My sister told me the whole story. I didn't want the story to become public, so I wrote to Mr Wickham. He left immediately. Mr Wickham wanted to marry my sister for her money.*

a housekeeper someone whose job is to look after a rich person's house

to run away to leave a place secretly to live with someone

Miss Bennet, this is the true story of my family's connection with Mr Wickham. Please believe everything I have said in this letter. Colonel Fitzwilliam knows the truth, if you want to ask him.
God bless you,

Fitzwilliam Darcy.'

◈◈◈

When Elizabeth started reading the letter, she felt a strong sense of prejudice. Mr Darcy had no reason to send her a letter. He couldn't say anything important to her. She was still angry when she finished Mr Darcy's comments about Jane. Then she started to read about Mr Wickham. 'This must be false,' she thought. Then she thought more carefully. All the information she had about Mr Wickham and Mr Darcy had come from Mr Wickham. It was true. Mr Wickham was very charming* and everybody liked him, but nobody really knew anything about him. Now Mr Wickham wanted to marry Miss King for money. Elizabeth had made a mistake. Mr Wickham was not a good man. She had been prejudiced. She thought again about the first part of Mr Darcy's letter. Everything was true. Jane didn't show her feelings, Mrs Bennet was embarrassing and Kitty and Lydia behaved badly.

Elizabeth walked around the countryside for two hours and then went home. Mrs Collins told her that Mr Darcy and Colonel Fitzwilliam had been to visit. They had come to say goodbye because they were returning to London. Elizabeth was happy that they were going away. All she could think about was the letter.

◈◈◈

charming nice and attractive

It was soon time for Elizabeth to return home to Longbourn. She enjoyed her last dinner at Rosings. Lady Catherine was as rude as usual. Elizabeth looked at Lady Catherine and thought to herself, 'Your nephew has asked me to marry him! You could be my aunt!' She laughed at the idea. Elizabeth now had mixed feelings about Mr Darcy. She was angry with herself and she was angry with her family. Mr Darcy was right.

◈◈◈

Elizabeth and Maria Lucas left Hunsford to spend a few days in London with the Gardiners, before going home with Jane. Elizabeth decided to say nothing to Jane until they arrived home at Longbourn.

The journey back to Meryton was very long. When they arrived, Kitty and Lydia had come to meet them in the village. They chatted about life in Meryton. They had two important pieces of news. They were sad because the militia were leaving; they were going to Brighton for the summer. They were happy because Miss King had left Meryton. 'Wickham is safe!' said Lydia happily.

'Perhaps Miss King is safe,' replied Elizabeth sharply.

Mrs Bennet was very happy to see Jane, as beautiful as ever, back in Longbourn. Mr Bennet was very happy to see Elizabeth back. Elizabeth was happy to be home, but worried about meeting Mr Wickham again.

◈◈◈

The next morning, Elizabeth told Jane about Mr Darcy's proposal. Jane was surprised, but pleased that Mr Darcy liked her sister. The two sisters also talked about Mr Wickham. They decided not to tell everyone in the village about Mr Wickham's true character, especially because the militia were leaving Meryton. Elizabeth didn't tell Jane about Mr Bingley because she didn't want Jane to be upset. While Jane and Elizabeth were talking, they could hear Lydia chatting excitedly to their mother. Lydia had just received an invitation from the militia colonel's wife to go to Brighton with her. Mrs Forster, was very young and had just married Colonel Forster. The colonel thought it would be a very good idea for his wife to have a young companion. Elizabeth was worried. She decided to speak to her father. 'I don't think Lydia should go to Brighton. She's too young. She behaves very badly. I've heard other people talk about how badly she behaves,' she said to Mr Bennet.

'Yes, Lizzy,' replied her father, 'but Lydia is a very silly girl. She won't be happy unless she goes to Brighton.'

'But father, she's vain*, lazy and ignorant. Going to Brighton will make her worse.'

'Don't worry, Lizzy. That will mean that people will like you and Jane more. They will see the difference between you and your silly younger sisters.'

Mr Bennet had decided. Lydia was going to Brighton.

◇◇◇

On the militia's last day in Meryton, Elizabeth saw Mr Wickham again. He asked Elizabeth about her time at Hunsford. She answered that she had seen Mr Darcy and his cousin Colonel Fitzwilliam at Rosings. 'How long were they at Rosings?' asked Mr Wickham.

'About three weeks.'

'Did you see them often?'

'Almost every day.'

'Colonel Fitzwilliam is a gentleman, unlike his cousin.'

vain proud of yourself or your appearance

'Oh, I think Mr Darcy is nicer, when you get to know him,' said Elizabeth.

Mr Wickham looked surprised. 'Perhaps he is happy about the marriage to Miss de Bourgh,' he said.

'Perhaps,' replied Elizabeth. She smiled to herself.

PET – Reading Comprehension

1 **Fill the gaps in Mr Darcy's letter to Elizabeth with the correct words - A, B, C or D.**

Dear Miss Bennet,

Do not be **(1)** ____ *, this is not another proposal of marriage. You must* **(2)** ____ *this letter. You are angry about Mr Bingley and your sister. You are also angry about Mr Wickham. I have some* **(3)** ____ *to say about both. First of all, I would like to explain* **(4)** ____ *Mr Bingley. When I was in Netherfield, I realised that Mr Bingley* **(5)** ____ *your sister very much. On the evening of the Netherfield ball, I saw that Charles* **(6)** ____ *in love with your sister. While you and I were* **(7)** ____, *Sir William Lucas* **(8)** ____ *to us. He said that Charles Bingley and your sister were going to get* **(9)** ____. *Everyone obviously thought this. I watched your sister for the rest of the evening. She smiled a lot, she was open and she was happy, but I saw no evidence that she was in love* **(10)** ____ *Charles. You said yesterday that she was very unhappy. I'm sorry about this. Perhaps I was wrong...*

	A	B	C	D
1	**A** afraid	**B** asked	**C** talked	**D** with
2	**A** write	**B** read	**C** eat	**D** arrive
3	**A** idea	**B** things	**C** one	**D** people
4	**A** you	**B** about	**C** for	**D** with
5	**A** liked	**B** found	**C** like	**D** love
6	**A** has	**B** had	**C** were	**D** was
7	**A** dance	**B** dancing	**C** dances	**D** danced
8	**A** spoke	**B** speaks	**C** speaking	**D** spoken
9	**A** marry	**B** marries	**C** married	**D** marrying
10	**A** for	**B** with	**C** to	**D** in

2 **Match the questions to the answers.**

1 ☐ What happened to Elizabeth on the road?
2 ☐ What did he give her?
3 ☐ What did Darcy's father want Mr Wickham to do?
4 ☐ What did Wickham and Miss Darcy plan to do?
5 ☐ How did Elizabeth feel after she read the letter?

6 ☐ How did Lady Catherine behave at dinner?
7 ☐ Why were Kitty and Lydia sad?
8 ☐ How did Mr Bennet feel about Elizabeth's return?
9 ☐ Why was Lydia excited?
10 ☐ What did Elizabeth think about Lydia?

a He wanted him to become a clergyman.
b He was very happy.
c Because the militia were going to Brighton.
d That going to Brighton would make her worse.
e She was as rude as usual.
f She'd been invited to Brighton.
g A letter.
h She realized she had made a mistake.
i She met Mr Darcy.
j They wanted to run away together.

Grammar

3 Past Perfect or Past Simple? Choose the correct alternative to complete these sentences.

1. Everything Elizabeth *had known/knew* about Mr Wickham and Mr Darcy *came/had come* from Mr Wickham.
2. Elizabeth *made/had made* a mistake, Mr Wickham *was not/had not been* a good man.
3. Elizabeth *had spoken/spoke* to the colonel for the first time. She *never met/had never met* him before.
4. When she *arrived/had arrived* at the parsonage, Mr Darcy and Colonel Fitzwilliam *already left/had already left.*
5. The two men had left. They *came/had come* to say goodbye before they *went/had gone* back to London.
6. Elizabeth *went/had gone* back to Longbourn once she *received/had received* the letter from Mr Darcy.
7. When they *had arrived/arrived*, they saw that Kitty and Lydia *had come/came* to meet them in the village.
8. They *were/had been* happy because Miss King *left/had left* Meryton.
9. Lydia *had been/was* happy because she *just received/had just received* an invitation to go to Brighton.
10. Elizabeth *had disagreed/disagreed*, but Mr Bennet *already decided/had already decided.*

4 -ing Form after Prepositions. If we use a verb after a preposition, we use the verb in its *-ing* form. Complete the sentences using the verbs in the box. Remember to put the verbs in their *-ing* form.

become • read • dance • sing • play • meet • be • travel

1 Kitty and Lydia were very fond of ____________.
2 Mary was very bad at ____________, but she often performed at balls.
3 Mr Wickham had no intention of ____________ a clergyman.
4 Elizabeth was worried about ____________ Mr Wickham.
5 Elizabeth was very excited about ____________ to Hunsford.
6 Mary was very serious. She was interested in ____________.
7 Miss Darcy was very good at ____________ the piano.
8 Charlotte Lucas was afraid of ____________ single all her life.

Speaking

5 Work in pairs. What are you

- fond of?
- bad at?
- worried about?
- excited about?
- interested in?
- good at?
- afraid of?

PRE-READING ACTIVITIES

PET – Listening

▶ 10 **6 Listen to the next part of the story. Choose the correct answer – A, B or C.**

1 Lydia went
A with Mrs Gardiner ☐
B with the militia ☐
C with Elizabeth ☐

2 Longbourn was quiet
A because everyone was away ☐
B because there were no parties ☐
C because it was the winter ☐

3 Elizabeth was	**A** worrying about her summer holiday	☐
	B enjoying her summer holiday	☐
	C looking forward to her summer holiday	☐
4 Mrs Gardiner was	**A** very excited	☐
	B very happy	☐
	C very worried	☐
5 It was	**A** a beautiful summer's day	☐
	B a dark stormy night	☐
	C a beautiful morning	☐
6 It took	**A** a few days to travel to Derbyshire	☐
	B a short time to travel to Derbyshire	☐
	C a long time to travel to Derbyshire	☐

PET – Writing

7 Your English teacher has asked you to write a story. Your story must end with this sentence:

Please believe me, I'm telling the truth.

Write your story in about 100 words.

Chapter Seven

Pemberley

10 The militia left Meryton as planned, and Lydia went with them. It was very quiet at Longbourn, with no parties or dinners. Elizabeth was looking forward to her summer holiday with her aunt and uncle Gardiner. She planned their trip to Derbyshire in her mind.

The day finally arrived and her Aunt and Uncle came to Longbourn. Mrs Gardiner was very excited too, because she had lived in Derbyshire when she was a girl and hadn't been there for many years.

They set off on their journey on a beautiful summer's day. It took a long time to travel to Derbyshire, but they stopped in places like Oxford and Birmingham on the way. Finally, they arrived in Lambton, the village where Mrs Gardiner had been born.

11 At dinner, that evening, they were planning the next day. 'You know, we're only five miles from Pemberley, Mr Darcy's estate,' said Mrs Gardiner, 'I think we should visit the house. I'm sure the housekeeper will let us look around.'

'But we aren't invited,' said Elizabeth, 'What if we meet Mr Darcy?'

'I asked the servant,' replied her aunt, 'The family is in London at the moment.'

The plan was made. Elizabeth was curious to see Mr Darcy's great estate.

The house at Pemberley was very large. The park and gardens were beautiful. In front of the house there was a river. Everything was perfect. 'If I married Mr Darcy, I would live here,' Elizabeth thought to herself.

Mr Gardiner spoke to the housekeeper. She was very happy to show them the house. Mr Darcy was away, she told them. 'He's arriving tomorrow with a group of friends,' she added.

Elizabeth was shocked. She really didn't want to meet Mr Darcy again. The housekeeper began to show them the house. 'Here is a picture of Mr Darcy,' she said.

'He's very handsome,' said Mrs Gardiner, 'I've never met him. Does he look like this Lizzy?'

Elizabeth replied, 'Yes. He's very handsome.'

The housekeeper was happy that Elizabeth knew Mr Darcy. 'He was such a kind child. I've known him since he was four years old. Some people say that he's proud, but I don't think that's true. I think he's quite shy. He's very generous and very good to the poor. And very kind to his sister. This is a picture of Miss Darcy.'

Elizabeth listened to the housekeeper. She wanted to hear more about Mr Darcy and his real character. Her aunt was quite surprised. 'This doesn't sound like Mr Darcy,' she whispered.

'No,' agreed Elizabeth, 'it doesn't. Perhaps we were wrong about Mr Wickham.'

When they had looked around the house, they thanked the housekeeper and went into the garden. They were walking along the path*. Elizabeth was a little in front of her uncle and aunt. Suddenly, Mr Darcy came round the corner. Their eyes met. They both blushed*. Elizabeth was very embarrassed and Mr Darcy was very surprised.

a path a small road for walking along

to blush to become red from embarrassment

'How is your family?' Mr Darcy asked.

'Very well, Sir, thank you.'

They spoke for a few minutes. They were both very polite, but very embarrassed. Then Mr Darcy said goodbye and walked into the house.

Mr and Mrs Gardiner continued their walk in the garden. Elizabeth was very confused. Mr Darcy had been kind and polite. 'Please let us go home,' she thought, 'This is a disaster.' But Mr and Mrs Gardiner were enjoying their walk.

A few minutes later, Elizabeth saw Mr Darcy walking towards them again. 'Do you like Pemberley?' he asked Elizabeth.

'Yes!' replied Elizabeth, 'It's a very beautiful house and your gardens are lovely too.'

'Will you introduce me to your friends?'

'Of course,' she said, as she introduced her uncle and aunt.

Mr Darcy talked to Mr Gardiner. They talked about the river and Mr Darcy invited Mr Gardiner to spend a day fishing at Pemberley. Elizabeth was very surprised. Mr Darcy wasn't proud at all. He was kind and interested, although the Gardiners were not rich or fashionable. After a while, Mr Darcy came to walk with Elizabeth. 'Miss Bennet,' he asked, 'can I introduce my sister to you while you are staying at Lambton? She's arriving at Pemberley tomorrow with Mr Bingley and his sisters.'

'Of course,' Elizabeth replied. She was surprised again. 'Is it possible that he still loves me?' she thought.

They returned to the carriage and Mr Darcy said goodbye. On the way back to Lambton, Mr and Mrs Gardiner talked about Mr Darcy. They liked him very much. 'He's not proud at all, just a little reserved,'

said Mrs Gardiner, 'I don't think we can trust Mr Wickham.'

◈◈◈

At ten o'clock the next morning, Mr Darcy arrived in Lambton with his sister. Elizabeth expected Miss Darcy to be very proud, but she was really very shy. Elizabeth liked her. They talked for a few minutes then Mr Darcy came back into the room with Mr Bingley. Mr Bingley was happy to see Elizabeth and asked about Jane. Elizabeth's visitors stayed for about half an hour. As they were leaving, Miss Darcy invited Elizabeth and the Gardiners to dinner at Pemberley, while they were staying in Lambton. That night, Elizabeth couldn't sleep. She was thinking about Mr Darcy. She didn't hate him. She was beginning to respect him. She was happy that he still loved her and that he wasn't angry with her.

◈◈◈

The following day, Mrs Gardiner and Elizabeth returned the visit to Miss Darcy at Pemberley. Caroline Bingley and her sister were there. Miss Darcy was very shy and Caroline and Louisa were unfriendly. Mr Darcy joined the ladies for tea. Caroline Bingley took the opportunity to embarrass Elizabeth. 'I believe Mr Wickham and the militia have left Meryton,' she said to Elizabeth, 'Your sisters must be very unhappy.'

It was an embarrassing moment for Mr Darcy and his sister. Poor Caroline didn't know about the unhappy love affair between Miss Darcy and Mr Wickham the summer before. Miss Darcy looked very shocked. Mr Darcy looked worried. But Elizabeth was very calm. She changed the subject and chatted about other things. Soon it was time for Elizabeth and Mrs Gardiner to leave.

When they had left, Caroline Bingley was very rude about

Elizabeth's appearance. 'She's never been very beautiful. She's very brown, not at all fashionable. And her eyes, well. I don't think they are particularly beautiful. You used to think she was quite pretty, didn't you, Mr Darcy?'

'Yes, I did. But that was only when I *first* met her,' replied Mr Darcy, 'Now I think she is the most beautiful woman I have ever met.' He left the room.

◈◈◈

Elizabeth had been expecting a letter from Jane, so she was very pleased the next morning, when two letters arrived for her. Mr and Mrs Gardiner went for walk, leaving Elizabeth to read her letters. They were both from Jane. Elizabeth opened the first letter. Jane had started writing the letter five days before. The first part of the letter was full of news about the family and the parties they had been to. The second part was not.

'...dearest Lizzy, something serious has happened. We had a letter from Colonel Forster in Brighton. Lydia has run away to Scotland. She's run away with one of his officers. Lydia has gone to Scotland with Mr Wickham! They are planning to get married. This is not a good marriage. Lydia is so young and we know Mr Wickham's character. I'll write again when I have more news.'

Elizabeth immediately opened the second letter. Jane had written it the day after the first letter.

'My dearest Lizzy, I have bad news. A marriage between Mr Wickham and Lydia would be a bad thing, but something worse has happened. They are not married. They didn't go to Scotland and

*Mr Wickham has no intention of marrying Lydia. We think they are living together in London. Colonel Forster says we can't trust Wickham. Poor Lydia. Mother is ill, she stays in her room all day. Father is going to London to look for Lydia. I hope they've got married in secret, but I don't think so. This will be a terrible scandal**. *None of us will ever find a husband. We must find them and make them get married. We need Mr Gardiner, he's so sensible** *and he knows London. Please come home!'*

Elizabeth jumped up from her chair and ran to the door. 'Uncle, uncle,' she shouted, 'Where is my uncle?'

But Mr Darcy was standing outside the door. 'Miss Bennet! What's the matter?' he cried, 'Are you ill?'

'I must find Mr Gardiner, I have urgent news.'

Mr Darcy called the servant. 'Find Mr Gardiner at once,' he shouted. 'Now, Miss Bennet, sit down,' he said, 'You are ill.'

'No. I'm not ill. I've just received some terrible news from Longbourn.'

Elizabeth began to cry. Mr Darcy didn't know what to do. 'Oh, Mr Darcy,' she cried, 'it's terrible news. My sister Lydia has left her family. She's left her friends, she's run away with Mr Wickham. She's lost forever.'

Mr Darcy was shocked. 'Is someone looking for her?' he cried.

'My father. It's my fault*! I knew about Mr Wickham's character, but I decided not to tell anyone.'

Mr Darcy was silent. He walked around the room. He was clearly very agitated*. Elizabeth watched him. She understood why he was agitated. He loved her and he wanted to marry her. She was in love with him. It was now impossible. The scandal of Lydia's behaviour

a scandal shocking news which people talk about
sensible practical
it's my fault I am responsible
agitated worried and upset

meant that none of the Bennet sisters would now find a husband. Mr Darcy eventually spoke. 'I must leave you. I must go. I'll tell my sister that you can't come to Pemberley today.'

'Thank you,' said Elizabeth, 'I'm very sorry. Please tell her that we have to leave urgently. Everyone will know the truth soon.'

'I'll never see him again,' thought Elizabeth sadly, as Mr Darcy walked out of the room.

Reading comprehension

1 Answer the questions – A, B or C.

1 Why is life quiet at Longbourn?
A because the militia have left ☐
B because Elizabeth has left ☐
C because Jane has left ☐

2 What does Mrs Gardiner suggest they do the next day?
A visit Mr Darcy ☐
B visit Pemberley ☐
C visit Mr Gardiner ☐

3 How does the housekeeper describe Mr Darcy?
A proud and arrogant ☐
B shy and generous ☐
C angry and silly ☐

4 How did Elizabeth and Darcy feel when they met unexpectedly?
A embarrassed and surprised ☐
B hot and cross ☐
C cold and distant ☐

5 Who is coming to Pemberley with Mr Bingley the following day?
A Mr Darcy's sister ☐
B Jane Bennet ☐
C Lydia Bennet ☐

6 How does Elizabeth feel about the news in Jane's letter?
A very angry ☐
B very happy ☐
C very upset ☐

7 What does Elizabeth think as Mr Darcy walks out of the room?
A that they will get married ☐
B that he is in love with her ☐
C that she will never see him again ☐

2 Match the pictures to the events in the story.

a Mr Bingley was happy to see Elizabeth and asked about Jane.

b Suddenly Mr Darcy came round the corner.

c It took a long time to travel to Derbyshire, but they stopped in places on the way.

d Elizabeth jumped from her chair and ran to the door.

e The house at Pemberley was very large. The park and gardens were beautiful.

f Elizabeth began to cry. Mr Darcy didn't know what to do.

g After a while, Mr Darcy came to walk with Elizabeth. 'Can I introduce my sister to you while you are at Lambton?' he asked.

h Mr and Mrs Gardiner went for a walk, leaving Elizabeth to read her letters.

Grammar

3 Phrasal Verbs. Read the sentences and match the phrasal verbs to their definitions.

1 The day before her wedding, Charlotte called on Elizabeth.
2 Elizabeth went back to Longbourn.
3 Elizabeth was looking forward to her holiday with the Gardiners.
4 They set off on their journey to Derbyshire.
5 Elizabeth and Mrs Gardiner looked around Pemberley.
6 Mr Darcy came into the room and sat down.
7 Lydia ran away to London with Mr Wickham.
8 Elizabeth took off her hat.

1 ☐ call on	**a** feel excited about
2 ☐ go back	**b** make yourself comfortable in a chair
3 ☐ look forward to	**c** visit a person
4 ☐ set off	**d** go to live with someone
5 ☐ look around	**e** remove
6 ☐ sit down	**f** return
7 ☐ run away	**g** start
8 ☐ take off	**h** visit a place

PET – Writing

4 Mixed Grammar Practice. Complete the second sentence so that it means the same as the first, using no more than three words.

1 We aren't very far away from Pemberley.
Pemberley .... here.

2 'I like Pemberley very much,' said Elizabeth.
Elizabeth said she .... very much.

3 If you don't practise every day, you won't improve.
You won't improve unless .... every day.

4 Why don't you marry Mr Darcy?
If I were you, ... marry Mr Darcy.

5 She is the most beautiful woman I have ever met.
I have never met a woman .... her.

Writing

5 **Imagine that you are Elizabeth Bennet or Mr Darcy. Write your diary for some of the events in Chapter Seven.**

August 15th

I arrived at Pemberley today. You can't imagine who I met.........

August 16th

August 17th

August 18th

Terrible news!.......

PRE-READING ACTIVITY

Speaking

6 **What do you think happens in the next chapter? Choose from the following options. Explain your reasons.**

- ☐ Lydia and Mr Wickham run away to live in France. They don't get married and there is a terrible scandal.
- ☐ Mr Bennet finds Mr Wickham in London. He fights Mr Wickham. Mr Wickham kills Mr Bennet.
- ☐ Mr Darcy writes a very cold letter to Elizabeth about the scandal in her family.
- ☐ Mr Wickham and Lydia get married in London. Mr Darcy helps them.

Chapter Eight

The Scandal

▶ 12 The Gardiners and Elizabeth returned to Longbourn immediately. On the journey, Elizabeth told them all about Mr Wickham's true character. Jane ran out to meet them as soon as the carriage arrived. 'Have you heard from father?' cried Elizabeth.

'Yes, but he can't find them,' said Jane sadly.

Mrs Bennet was upstairs in her room. She seemed worried about her husband, but she was really worried about herself. 'What if Mr Bennet fights Mr Wickham?' she said, 'Mr Wickham will kill him, then Mr Collins will inherit Longbourn and we'll have to leave. Where will we go?'

Mary Bennet was very shocked at Lydia's behaviour. She spent a lot of time reading religious books and talked a lot about Lydia's immorality*. Kitty was very quiet. Jane suspected that Lydia had probably told Kitty about her plans in a letter.

Mr and Mrs Gardiner stayed for lunch, but then left for London. Mr Gardiner wanted to help Mr Bennet as soon as possible.

◈◈◈

The next day, a messenger* arrived with a letter. Everyone hoped it was a letter from Mr Bennet, but it was from Mr Collins. The letter was addressed to Mr Bennet, but Jane decided to open it. Mrs Bennet was still in her room, so Jane read the letter to her sisters.

immorality behaviour that is wrong

a messenger someone who brings a letter

'My dear sir,

Mrs Collins and I are very sorry to hear about your daughter. Her death would be preferable to this. My wife says that Lydia has always been out of your control. I think she must be very bad. Lady Catherine is also very sorry. She says that none of your daughters will get married now, because no-one will want such scandal in their family. I think you should forget Lydia forever...'

A letter came from Mr Gardiner the next day. He said that Wickham had very bad debts* in Brighton. He played cards for money and he often lost. This was the reason Wickham had run away. Nobody could find Mr Wickham and Lydia. Mr Gardiner also said that Mr Bennet was leaving London.

◈◈◈

Mr Bennet arrived home the day after. He was very upset. 'Are they in London?' Elizabeth asked him.

'Probably,' said Mr Bennet sadly. He went into his study and closed the door.

Later that afternoon, Mr Bennet joined the girls in the sitting room. 'Lizzy,' he said, 'I want to say something. You were right. It was a bad idea to allow Lydia to go to Brighton. I've been a bad father. I made a mistake.

'Kitty,' he continued, 'I have learnt from my mistake. No officer is ever going to enter my house again. You will *not* be allowed to go to balls, unless you dance with one of your sisters. And you will spend more time on study.'

Kitty began to cry.

◈◈◈

a bad debt money that he has lost by playing cards and needs to pay

Two days later, a letter came for Mr Bennet. It was from Mr Gardiner.

'My dear Brother-in-law,
I've found Lydia and I've spoken to her and to Mr Wickham. They aren't married. I don't think it was Mr Wickham's intention ever to marry Lydia. I think, however, there's a way to make them marry. If you'll pay them £100 a year and if Lydia receives her inheritance of £1,000 when you die, then Wickham will marry her. It seems that he still has some friends who will help them. Don't come to London, I'll arrange everything.'

The Bennets all reacted differently to the news. 'They must marry,' said Mr Bennet, 'but I don't like my future son-in-law. I think Mr Gardiner has paid this man to marry my daughter.'

'My Lydia's getting married!' cried Mrs Bennet, 'And she's only just sixteen. But I must go to London to buy wedding clothes. Oh what a handsome husband she has! Mrs Wickham. That's such a good name!'

'How are we going to pay all Wickham's debts?' said Elizabeth.

'We must try to forget everything,' said Jane, 'I hope they will be very happy.'

◈◈◈

A few weeks later, the newly-married Mr and Mrs Wickham visited Longbourn. They were on their way to the north of England. Mr Wickham was joining the army there. Lydia was just the same, she chatted, laughed and joked. Mr Wickham was as charming as usual. They were not embarrassed about their behaviour at all. Jane and Elizabeth were shocked. Mr Bennet was very cold to them. Mrs

Bennet was different. She was very pleased with her new son-in-law. She visited all her neighbours with Lydia to show them her married daughter. Elizabeth tried to avoid spending time with Lydia and her husband, but one morning, Lydia came to talk to her. 'I never told you about my wedding,' she said.

'I don't think you should talk about it,' Elizabeth replied. 'I don't like the way you found your husband.'

But Lydia wanted to tell the story of her wedding, so she continued. 'We got married at eleven. There weren't many people there. Wickham's friends from the militia couldn't come, so there was only my aunt and uncle and Mr Darcy.'

'Mr Darcy?' cried Elizabeth, 'Was Mr Darcy there?'

'I forgot!' replied Lydia, 'It's a big secret. Don't tell my husband. He said I must never tell anyone that Mr Darcy was at our wedding.'

Elizabeth wrote a letter to her aunt that evening. She wanted to know why Mr Darcy had been at her sister's wedding. Mrs Gardiner sent a reply immediately.

Dear Lizzy,
Thank you for your letter. I'm very surprised that you didn't know about Mr Darcy and Wickham. Mr Gardiner is also surprised. We thought you would know. Let me tell you immediately:
The day after we came back from Longbourn, your uncle had a visitor. It was Mr Darcy. It seems Mr Darcy left Derbyshire when we did and went to London. He found Wickham and Lydia. He decided to pay Wickham to marry Lydia. He came to your uncle to explain the situation. Mr Darcy is a very generous man. He is not proud, but he is a little bit stubborn. He wanted to pay all Wickham's debts too. Everyone thinks your uncle paid, because Mr Darcy asked us to keep*

stubborn not happy to change your ideas about things

this secret. Now you know and I'm very happy. I think Mr Darcy did this because he loves you. He didn't talk about you, but I hope you'll get married one day. I'm looking forward to walking around Pemberley, when I come to stay...'

Elizabeth was very happy. Mr Darcy had helped Lydia and the Bennet family. Mr Darcy had been very generous to them all. Mr Darcy was still in love with her! While she was thinking, Mr Wickham came to talk to her. 'I believe you visited Pemberley, when you were in Derbyshire,' he said.

'Yes, I did.'

'Did you meet Miss Darcy?'

'Yes,' replied Elizabeth, 'I liked her very much.'

'Mmm. A friend told me that she had improved this last year. Did you see the church at Pemberley, the church intended for me?'

'Yes, I did. I also heard that you decided not to join the church and that Mr Darcy gave you money instead.'

Mr Wickham was silent. He never spoke to Elizabeth about it again.

◈◈◈

Soon, Mr and Mrs Wickham left Longbourn for the north. Everyone was happy to see them go, except for Mrs Bennet. Life was very quiet at Longbourn until the Bennets received some news.

'Mr Bingley is coming back to Netherfield!' said Aunt Phillips one day. 'He's coming with a party of gentlemen.'

'I don't care,' said Mrs Bennet, 'Mr Bingley means nothing to us.'

◈◈◈

A few days later, Mrs Bennet and her daughters were in the sitting room, when they heard the sound of horses outside. Kitty went to the window. 'It's Mr Bingley,' she said, 'and that other man. The tall, proud one.'

'Mr Darcy!' said her mother, 'Mr Bingley is welcome here. His friends are welcome too, but I don't like Mr Darcy at all.'

The two gentlemen came into the sitting room. Mrs Bennet was very polite to Mr Bingley. She was extremely rude to Mr Darcy.

Mrs Bennet talked about Lydia's marriage to Mr Wickham the whole time. Mrs Bennet thought that her daughter's marriage was a triumph. Elizabeth was very embarrassed; she had kept Mr Darcy's secret, so Mrs Bennet didn't know how Mr Darcy had helped Lydia. Mr Bingley and Mr Darcy seemed embarrassed too. Mr Darcy said very little during the visit. As the gentlemen were leaving, Mrs Bennet invited them to dinner the following Tuesday.

◈◈◈

On Tuesday evening, there was a large dinner party at Longbourn. Mr Bingley sat next to Jane. They smiled and talked together all evening. Mr Darcy sat near Mrs Bennet. Elizabeth could see that they talked very little. They were very cold to each other. Elizabeth wanted to talk to Mr Darcy, but she had no opportunity. She really wanted to thank Mr Darcy for his kindness to Lydia. She also wanted to apologize for her mother's very rude behaviour.

◈◈◈

A few days after the dinner party, Mr Bingley called again. He was alone, because Mr Darcy had gone back to London. The following morning, Mr Bingley called again, very early in the morning. This time, Mrs Bennet made sure that he and Jane had some time alone together. Mr Bingley asked Jane to marry him and Jane agreed. Mr Bingley went to ask Mr Bennet's permission. Everyone at Longbourn was delighted. Elizabeth was very happy for her sister and Mr Bennet liked Mr Bingley. Mrs Bennet was sure they would be very happy because Mr Bingley was so rich. Everyone in Meryton said that the Bennets were the luckiest family in the world. Just a few weeks before, when Lydia had run away, everyone had said the opposite.

Reading Comprehension

1 Match the questions to the answers.

1 ☐ What does Mrs Bennet think will happen if Mr Bennet fights Mr Wickham?
2 ☐ What does Mr Collins say in his letter?
3 ☐ Why has Wickham run away from Brighton?
4 ☐ What does Mr Bennet say to Kitty?
5 ☐ Why are Jane and Elizabeth shocked by Wickham and Lydia?
6 ☐ Why does Elizabeth write to her aunt?
7 ☐ How does Elizabeth feel about Mr Darcy's generosity and help?
8 ☐ Who comes to visit the Bennets?
9 ☐ How does Mrs Bennet feel about Mr Darcy?
10 ☐ What does Mr Bingley say to Jane?

a That she can never go to a ball again.
b Mr Bingley and Mr Darcy.
c Because she wants to know why Mr Darcy was at Lydia's wedding.
d He asks her to marry him.
e Because he plays cards for money and often loses.
f That Mr Bennet will die and Mr Collins will inherit Longbourn.
g She doesn't like him and she's rude to him.
h Because they aren't embarrassed about their behaviour.
i She's very happy that he is still in love with her.
j That Lydia must be very bad.

PET – Reading

2 Fill the gaps in Mrs Gardiner's letter to Elizabeth with the correct word – A, B, C or D.

Dear Lizzy,

Thank you for your **(1)** _____ *. I'm very surprised that you didn't know* **(2)** ____ *Mr Darcy and Wickham. Mr Gardiner is also surprised.*

*We **(3)** ____ you would know. Let me **(4)** ____ you immediately. The day after we **(5)** ____ back from Longbourn, your uncle had a visitor. It was Mr Darcy. It seems Mr Darcy left Derbyshire when we did and **(6)** ____ to London. He found Wickham and Lydia. He decided to pay Wickham to **(7)** ____ Lydia. He came to your uncle to **(8)** ____ the situation. Mr Darcy is a very generous man. He is not proud, but he is a little bit stubborn. He wanted to pay all Wickham's debts too. Everyone thinks your uncle paid, because Mr Darcy **(9)** ____ us to keep this secret. Now you know and I'm very happy. I think Mr Darcy **(10)** ____ this because he loves you. He didn't talk about you, but I hope you'll get married one day. I'm looking forward to walking around Pemberley when I come to stay...*

1	**A** friend	**B** asked	**C** letter	**D** writing
2	**A** for	**B** about	**C** with	**D** to
3	**A** think	**B** thing	**C** thinking	**D** thought
4	**A** tell	**B** say	**C** told	**D** said
5	**A** came	**B** found	**C** come	**D** find
6	**A** has	**B** had	**C** were	**D** went
7	**A** dance	**B** talk	**C** married	**D** marry
8	**A** explain	**B** explained	**C** explaining	**D** explanation
9	**A** said	**B** asked	**C** says	**D** asking
10	**A** had	**B** was	**C** did	**D** made

Grammar

3 Time Expressions.
Choose the best time expression from the two alternatives in the text.

While/During the journey back to Longbourn, Elizabeth told the Gardiners all about Mr Wickham. She explained about what had happened between Mr Wickham and Miss Darcy *the year before/Tuesday*. *During/As soon as* they arrived at Longbourn, Jane ran out to meet them. She said that a letter had come from Mr Bennet *Thursday week/the day before*. Mr Gardiner left for London because he wanted to help Mr Bennet *while/as soon as possible*. Mr Bennet arrived home *as soon as/the day after*. Nobody could find Lydia and Wickham. *The year before/A few weeks later,* the newly-married Mr and Mrs Wickham visited Longbourn.

4 Question Forms. Write questions for these answers. Be careful, the tenses are mixed!

1 How long ____?
They only stayed a few days.

2 How ____?
Elizabeth travelled back by carriage.

3 Where ____?
Lydia and Mr Wickham were probably in London.

4 What ____?
Elizabeth asked her aunt a question.

5 Who ____?
Mr Darcy helped Lydia.

6 Who ____?
I met Miss Darcy.

7 When ____?
Mr Bingley came to visit a few days later.

8 Why ____?
Elizabeth was embarrassed because her mother was rude to Mr Darcy.

Vocabulary

5 Use your dictionary to find the meanings of the words in the box. Then insert the words into the sentences below.

bride • wedding • bridegroom • rings • wedding dress honeymoon • bouquet • reception

1 When people get married, they often exchange __________.

2 The woman who is getting married is called a __________.

3 The man who is getting married is called a __________.

4 The ceremony is called a __________.

5 The woman usually wears a __________.

6 The woman sometimes carries a __________.

7 After the ceremony, there is often a party called a __________.

8 The newly-married couple often go on holiday. The holiday is called a __________.

Speaking

6 **Work in pairs. Talk about different types of weddings in your country. Think about**

- clothes
- food
- the ceremony

Writing

7 **Use the notes about Mr Darcy below to write a description of him. Use your own ideas too.**

Appearance: *tall, handsome*
Status in life: *rich, a gentleman, has a large estate*
Family: *sister - Georgiana, aunt – Lady Catherine de Bourgh*
Character: *proud or shy? kind or horrible? intelligent or silly?*

PRE-READING ACTIVITY

Speaking

8 **How would you like the story to end? Work in pairs to talk about a good ending. Use these questions to help you.**

- What does Lady Catherine de Bourgh do at the beginning of the next chapter?
- Should there be a happy ending or a sad ending?
- Should anyone get married at the end? Who?

Chapter Nine

An Unexpected Visitor

▶ 13 About a week after Mr Bingley's engagement, an enormous carriage arrived at Longbourn. Kitty looked out of the window, but she didn't recognize the carriage or the lady who got out of it. The unexpected visitor came into the sitting room. It was Lady Catherine de Bourgh. She sat down without saying a word. She looked around the room. She was even ruder than usual. 'I imagine *that* lady is your mother,' said Lady Catherine.

'Yes,' replied Elizabeth.

Mrs Bennet was so shocked at having such a great lady in the house that she couldn't think of anything to say.

'And I imagine *that* is one of your sisters.'

'Yes,' said Mrs Bennet, who had recovered*, 'she is my second youngest daughter. My youngest was married recently.'

'Hmm. You have a very small park here and this is a very hot room.'

'Would you like some refreshments*?' asked Mrs Bennet very politely.

'No,' said Lady Catherine very rudely.

After a few uncomfortable minutes, Lady Catherine said to Elizabeth, 'Come outside for a walk with me.'

Elizabeth followed her into the garden.

'Miss Bennet,' she began, 'I think you know why I'm here.'

to recover to feel better

refreshments something to eat or drink

'No,' Elizabeth replied. 'It's a pleasure to see you, but I don't know why you've come.'

'Miss Bennet! Do not lie* to me. I've heard that you are to marry my nephew, Mr Darcy. My nephew! This is, of course, impossible. Has my nephew asked you to marry him?'

'You've said that it's impossible,' said Elizabeth, who was quite shocked.

'It *is* impossible. He is going to marry *my daughter.*'

'If he's engaged to Miss de Bourgh, then Mr Darcy will not marry me. What's the problem?'

'His mother and I planned their engagement. They will marry each other.'

'Mr Darcy will decide for himself,' said Elizabeth angrily.

'He *cannot* marry you!'

'Why? My father's a gentleman.'

'Who's your mother? Who are your uncles and aunts? Your sister ran away with a soldier. Everybody knows about her marriage – it's a scandal. You aren't good enough for my nephew. You aren't good enough for Pemberley!'

Elizabeth was offended. She started to walk away. But Lady Catherine had another question. 'Tell me now! Are you engaged to my nephew?' she asked angrily.

'No, I am not,' replied Elizabeth coldly.

Lady Catherine was pleased. 'Good, and will you promise never to marry my nephew?'

'No!' said Elizabeth firmly. 'I will not. I'm going back to the house.'

Lady Catherine was now furious. She walked quickly towards her

to lie to say something that isn't true

carriage. 'You will not marry my nephew. I'll stop you.' She got into the carriage and it drove away.

Elizabeth went back into the house.

'She is a very fine lady, but why did she come here? Did Lady Catherine come to bring a message from Charlotte?' asked Mrs Bennet.

'Yes,' lied Elizabeth, 'Mr and Mrs Collins are both well.'

◈◈◈

The following day, Mr Bennet had a letter from Mr Collins. He called Elizabeth into his study.

'Mr Collins says that you are getting married!' he said. 'Mr Collins is sure that you are getting married to *Mr Darcy!* And he says that Lady Catherine is not happy about this. Is that why she came here yesterday?' Mr Bennet was laughing, 'I know you don't like Mr Darcy. Nobody likes Mr Darcy! Oh, Lizzy, Mr Collins is a very silly man.'

Elizabeth pretended that it was funny. She laughed with her father, but she felt different. She now hoped that Mr Darcy still wanted to marry her.

◈◈◈

A few days later, Mr Bingley came to Longbourn with Mr Darcy. Mr Bingley suggested that they all go out for a walk. Mr Bennet was reading in his study, Mrs Bennet didn't like walking and Mary didn't have time. She was reading a book of sermons*. Jane, Elizabeth and Kitty all agreed to go out together. Jane and Bingley walked ahead together, and Mr Darcy, Elizabeth and Kitty walked slowly behind, so that Jane and Mr Bingley had the chance to talk. Kitty was afraid of Mr Darcy because he was such a fine gentleman, so she said very little.

sermons religious talks

When they arrived at Sir William Lucas's house, Kitty went to call on Maria, leaving Elizabeth and Darcy alone.

'I'm sorry, Mr Darcy,' said Elizabeth, 'but I've wanted to talk to you for a very long time. I want to thank you for your kindness to Lydia and to my family.'

'I'm sorry,' replied Darcy, 'That should be a secret. I'm surprised Mrs Gardiner has told you.'

'It's my fault,' said Elizabeth, 'Lydia said that you were at her wedding. I asked Mrs Gardiner to tell me and she explained everything. I want to thank you for myself and my family.'

'Please thank me for yourself. I was only thinking about you. I respect your family, but I did this for you.'

They walked in silence for a while. 'Miss Bennet,' said Mr Darcy suddenly, 'do you feel the same as you felt last Easter? My feelings are the same, I still want to marry you.'

'No,' replied Elizabeth, 'my feelings are very different from last Easter. In fact, I feel the opposite. I love you.'

Mr Darcy was delighted.

They talked about the evening at Hunsford last Easter, when Mr Darcy had proposed. They agreed that they had both changed. Mr Darcy was less proud and less reserved, Elizabeth was less prejudiced. Mr Darcy then explained why Mr Bingley had come back to Netherfield. 'I told him Jane was in love with him,' he said.

Mr Darcy and Elizabeth continued on their walk. They talked about their love and they talked about marriage.

◆◆◆

The next evening, Mr Darcy came to talk to Mr Bennet. They talked in the study for some time. Mr Darcy immediately left the house and

Mr Bennet called Elizabeth. 'He wants to marry you. He says you want to marry him. Are you mad?' said Mr Bennet, 'Why do you want to marry this man?'

'I love him.'

'Are you sure? I know he's rich, I believe he has even more money than Mr Bingley. But I don't want you to be unhappy. He's proud and unpleasant, but if you really love him…'

'I love him, father,' interrupted Elizabeth, 'He isn't proud at all. I will be very happy with him.'

'Well, congratulations!' said Mr Bennet, 'I'm very happy for you.'

Elizabeth told him what Mr Darcy had done for Lydia. Mr Bennet was very pleased. Mrs Bennet was totally silent when she heard the news. It didn't take long for her to change her mind about Mr Darcy. 'Oh, what good news! I have always liked Mr Darcy. He has ten thousand pounds a year. Three of my girls married!' she cried. She was delighted.

◈◈◈

A few days later, Mr Darcy and Elizabeth were talking about their wedding. 'When did you fall in love with me?' asked Elizabeth suddenly.

'I don't know. I have always loved your lively mind,' replied Mr Darcy.

'I think I was different from the other women you knew. They all wanted to marry you, but I didn't! But when did you realize that I loved you?'

'When Lady Catherine told me about your conversation with her,' replied Darcy, 'Poor Lady Catherine gave me hope!'

'Have you told Lady Catherine that we are getting married?' asked Elizabeth innocently.

'I'll write to her!' said Mr Darcy.

◈◈◈

People's reactions to the two engagements were very different. Caroline Bingley was very unhappy, but she wrote a loving, if insincere, letter to her brother and another to Jane. Jane wrote a very kind reply, although she never really trusted Caroline again. Mr and Mrs Gardiner were very happy for Jane and for Elizabeth and Miss Darcy was very happy too. She wrote a long letter of congratulations to her brother. Mr Collins was not very happy. He and Charlotte came to stay with Charlotte's mother and father. They had decided not to be near Rosings Park at the moment, because Lady Catherine was so angry. She blamed Mrs Collins for being a friend of Elizabeth's and Mr Collins for being her cousin. Lady Catherine's reply to Mr Darcy's letter was not pleasant either. She wrote a very rude letter and was very unkind about Elizabeth. Mr Darcy didn't speak to her for a very long time.

◈◈◈

Miss Jane Bennet married Mr Charles Bingley on the same day as her sister, Miss Elizabeth Bennet, married Mr Fitzwilliam Darcy. It was the happiest day of Mrs Bennet's life.

The two marriages were very happy. Elizabeth and Darcy spent a lot of their time at Pemberley. They were very happy in Derbyshire and Elizabeth loved the house and its gardens.

After their wedding, Jane and Mr Bingley stayed at Netherfield for about a year. Netherfield was, perhaps, too near to Mrs Bennet and

her relations in Meryton, so Mr Bingley bought an estate in the north of England. Fortunately, it was very near to Pemberley and Jane and Elizabeth visited each other often.

Mrs Bennet herself was proud of her three sons-in-law and the fact that three of her daughters were married, but Mr Wickham was always her favourite. She remained a silly woman.

Mr Bennet missed his second daughter very much. He often visited Pemberley to stay with Elizabeth and her husband.

As for the younger Bennet sisters; Kitty spent a lot of her time staying with either Jane or Elizabeth and became a fine young woman. Mary was the only daughter who stayed at home. She now had less time to spend reading and practising her music, because her mother needed her company more. Lydia and Wickham stayed in the north of England. They were often short of money, but Elizabeth sent them a little now and again. Their marriage was very unhappy. Mr Darcy never invited Mr Wickham to stay at Pemberley, but Lydia sometimes visited Pemberley when Mr Darcy was away. Lydia often went to stay with Mr Bingley and Jane, but she always stayed too long.

Caroline Bingley was shocked when Mr Darcy married Elizabeth. She had wanted to marry Mr Darcy herself. She decided to be nice to Elizabeth so she could still visit the Darcys at Pemberley.

Miss Georgiana Darcy lived with Mr Darcy and Elizabeth at Pemberley. Mr Darcy was very pleased that Georgiana and Elizabeth were such good friends. Elizabeth had a very good influence on Georgiana. She became much less shy, although she was surprised at the lively way Elizabeth sometimes disagreed with Mr Darcy.

What about Lady Catherine de Bourgh? Mr Darcy was very angry about Lady Catherine's letter. A few years later, Mr Darcy wrote to her. It was Elizabeth's idea. Eventually, Lady Catherine came to stay at Pemberley. She was as rude as ever.

Elizabeth and Mr Darcy were always very happy when Mr and Mrs Gardiner came to stay. Mr Darcy and Elizabeth both liked Elizabeth's uncle and aunt because, after all, they had brought Elizabeth to Derbyshire and united the happy couple.

The End

Reading Comprehension

1 Answer the questions, true (T) or false (F). Correct the false answers.

	T	F
1 Mrs Collins arrives at Longbourn in an enormous carriage.	☐	☐
2 Mrs Bennet is very shocked.	☐	☐
3 Lady Catherine de Bourgh asks Mrs Bennet to go for a walk.	☐	☐
4 Elizabeth promises never to marry Lady Catherine's nephew.	☐	☐
5 Elizabeth lies to her mother about the reason for Lady Catherine's visit.	☐	☐
6 Elizabeth feels the same about Mr Darcy as she did last Easter.	☐	☐
7 Mr Bennet thinks Elizabeth is mad to want to marry Mr Darcy.	☐	☐
8 Caroline Bingley is happy that Elizabeth and Mr Darcy are getting married.	☐	☐
9 Jane and Elizabeth get married on the same day.	☐	☐
10 Lady Catherine never comes to stay at Pemberley.	☐	☐

Vocabulary

2 **Choose the best time expression from the two alternatives in the text.**

First of all/Later Mr Darcy thought that Elizabeth was only quite pretty. *Then/Before that* he realized that she was beautiful and *next/first of all* he fell in love with her. He went to stay with his aunt, Lady Catherine de Bourgh and *secondly/after that* he asked Elizabeth to marry him. She said no and he didn't see her again until the summer when they met at Pemberley. *First of all/Finally*, when he came back to Netherfield with Mr Bingley, Mr Darcy and Elizabeth agreed to get married.

Writing

3 **You work for a newspaper, The Meryton Times. Write a report about the story of Pride and Prejudice for your readers. Use these notes about the plot to help you. Remember to add information about the characters.**

Autumn

Bingley & Darcy at Netherfield, Bennet sisters meet them, Jane ill
Mr Collins proposes to Elizabeth, then Charlotte
Mr Wickham comes to Meryton

Winter

Mr Bingley leaves
Jane goes to London
Elizabeth goes to Hunsford

Spring

Darcy proposes, Elizabeth refuses

Summer

Elizabeth meets Mr Darcy at Pemberley
Lydia runs away with Mr Wickham

Autumn

Mr Wickham & Lydia get married
Mr Bingley engaged to Jane
Lady Catherine comes to Longbourn
Mr Darcy engaged to Elizabeth
Double wedding

Jane Austen

Early Life

Jane Austen was born on 16th December 1775 in Steventon, a small village in the south of England. Her father was a clergyman and he was a very kind, handsome man. Her mother was beautiful and all the Austen children were very good-looking like their parents.

Jane was the seventh of the eight children. She had six brothers but only one sister, Cassandra, who was two years older. The two sisters were great friends.

Education

When Cassandra was going away to school, Jane wanted to go too. She was only 6, but she was so angry about being without her sister, that the family agreed she could go. School finished when Jane was only 11, then her father educated her. Their library at home was full of books and Jane loved reading, like all the Austen children.

The Writer

Jane started writing when she was only ten or eleven years old. One of her early books was a comical look at history. It was in the style of a bad historian. She called it The History of England by a Partial Prejudiced and Ignorant Historian. Cassandra drew pictures of the people. One of the funniest is of Henry VIII wearing a red nightcap*. They thought it was the right kind of picture for a man who had had six wedding nights!

Jane wrote books all her life, but the first of her novels to be published was Sense and Sensibility in 1811. The book was published without Jane's name on the cover. The book simply said 'By a Lady'. At that time, it was still very unusual for women to publish books. Emma was the first book to have Jane's name on its cover. Jane's last two novels were published after her death.

Love

Jane Austen never married. She wanted to marry for love, so she waited for the right man to come along. One story says that she fell in love with a man while she was on holiday at the seaside. Tragically for Jane, he died very suddenly. When Jane was twenty-six, a friend of her brother's proposed to her. Twenty-six was considered quite old at the time and she accepted him. The engagement lasted less than twenty-four hours. The following morning, Jane realised that she didn't love the man and she ended her engagement to him.

The Novels

Sense and Sensibility 1811
Pride and Prejudice 1813
Mansfield Park 1814
Emma 1816
Northanger Abbey 1818
Persuasion 1818

Later Years

After moving to different places in England, in 1809 Jane moved to a cottage in Chawton with her mother and sister. Jane was very happy there. She spent a lot of her time gardening, making wine and writing. She also loved being an aunt to all her nieces and nephews and they loved her. When she was only 41, Jane fell ill. She died in Cassandra's arms, on 18th July 1817, in Winchester.

Task

Complete the form with the information about Jane Austen.

Name: ______________________
Place of birth: ______________________
Date of birth: ______________________
Father's occupation: ______________________
Number of brothers and sisters: ______________________
Age started school: ______________________
Age left school: ______________________
Occupation: ______________________
Name and date of first publication: ______________________
Names of most famous novels: ______________________
Date of death: ______________________
Age when died: ______________________

a nightcap a hat you wear in bed

Everyday Life in Jane Austen's Times

Society and Social Customs

In Jane Austen's world, society was divided into three main groups: the aristocracy, the gentry and the common people. Jane Austen mainly wrote about the gentry, who included people with land and clergymen. In Pride and Prejudice, Lady Catherine de Bourgh is an aristocrat, Mr Darcy and Elizabeth are from the gentry and Mrs Bennet's relations are common people.

London

Aristocrats usually had a house in London and an estate in the country. Aristocrats and members of the gentry often spent some time in London every year, so that they could go to fashionable balls and parties. This was mainly so that they could meet people of the opposite sex who came from their own social class. People who didn't go to London went to local balls and parties.

Dancing

Jane Austen was a very good dancer, so she loved going to dances. Dancing at the time was very formal, the lady and the gentleman danced far away from each other. There was, however, a new dance from Germany, a scandalous dance called the waltz. This dance was shocking because the couple held each other quite closely and even looked into each other's eyes! People in polite society didn't dance it.

Men and Women

Men and women couldn't meet freely as they can today. If a woman was 'out' she was able to go to dances, balls and parties. The reason for being out was really to meet a man to marry. It was quite normal for younger sisters not to go to parties and balls until their older sisters were married. When they were married, women could be chaperones* for their sisters.

Walking

People often went for a walk during the day. When people visited London, they usually walked in the Royal Parks and public gardens. A man and a woman could only walk together if they were married or brother and sister, so people often went for a walk in large groups. The big parks often put on entertainment, such as music and plays.

Playing Cards

A lot of people played cards. When people went to balls, they didn't dance all the time. It was quite common for both men and women to play cards. In London, fashionable people often played in public for money. Some aristocrats lost thousands and thousands of pounds and had to sell their estates to pay their debts.

Other Pastimes

Shopping was an important pastime during the day, when people visited important cities. This was when people bought material for making clothes, jewellery, books and objects for the house. Jane Austen enjoyed shopping when she was in London.

People also went to the theatre, which was very popular entertainment in London and Bath. People didn't go out a lot, so a lot of entertainment was at home. Music was very important to both the aristocracy and the gentry. Women usually played the piano and men and women both sang. Conversation was also very important.

Task

Write a paragraph about modern society and social customs. Think about how men and women meet, what people do for entertainment, what games people play and what other pastimes they have.

chaperone someone who looked after an unmarried woman at parties and on walks

Dangerous and Exciting Times

Jane Austen lived in a period of great world change. Remember that she was born in 1775 and died in 1817.

Social Changes

There were lots of reasons for changes in the social structure. One reason is that more and more people were making money from 'trade*'. In Pride and Prejudice, Mr Gardiner is an example of this. He doesn't come from the gentry, but he has enough money to have a very comfortable life in London. He has a servant and he has a carriage. During Jane Austen's lifetime, a lot of people from trade married people from the gentry. All through Jane Austen's life, the Industrial Revolution was happening in Britain. This had an effect on cities like London, but also on the countryside. People began to move away from the countryside to new cities like Manchester and Birmingham for work.

Changes in the Lives of Women

As you can see from *Pride and Prejudice*, women from the gentry were mainly concerned with marriage and their family. Miss Darcy was very rich, but her money would go to her husband when she got married. Jane Austen was one of the first women writers, but didn't publish her first books with her own name. *Pride and Prejudice* simply said written 'By a Lady'.

Inventions

Here are some of the things which were invented during Jane Austen's lifetime and their effects.

1775 Steam ship* (Jacques Perrier), made sea travel faster.

1776 Submarine (David Bushnell), important for exploration.

1800 Electric battery (Alessandro Volta), the first practical battery.

1804 Steam locomotive (Richard Trevithick), important for transport.

1807 Conveyor belt* (Oliver Evans), important for industrialization.

1810 Canning* (Nicolas Appert), made it possible to keep food longer.

1812 Photographic lens* (William Wollaston), important for publishing and entertainment.

1816 Bicycle (Karl von Sauerbronn), important for transport and entertainment.

World Changes

Here are just some of the events that happened in Jane Austen's lifetime:

1776 The United States Declaration of Independence, when the American colonies broke away from Britain.

1789 The French Revolution began. This had a very profound effect on the social structure all over Europe.

1793 France declared war on Britain, Holland and Spain. For most of Jane Austen's life, Britain was at war with France and Napoleon.

1807 The end of the slave* trade in Britain. People had been fighting to stop the slave trade for more than twenty years.

Task

Make a list of all the important events that have happened in your lifetime. Think about social changes, wars and inventions.

____

____

____

____

____

trade buying or selling things
steam ship a boat that is powered by the vapour which comes from boiling water
conveyor belt a way of moving things around a factory
canning the process of putting food into cans/tins
lens the part of the camera that you look through
a slave someone who belongs to another person

Travelling

Travelling in Jane Austen's time was very difficult. She was writing just before the coming of trains and railways, so most travel was by road. It's important to remember that 90% of the population never left the place where they were born and only the rich could travel long distances. Most people walked and it was quite normal for people to walk ten kilometres to work in the morning and ten kilometres home.

Means of Transport

People from the gentry and the aristocracy usually travelled by carriage. Carriages were pulled by different numbers of horses, depending on how much money you had or how long your journey was. Sometimes people used public carriages to travel long distances. It took a long time. Today you can travel from London to Edinburgh by train in about five hours. In the nineteenth century, it took twelve days to get from London to Edinburgh and the carriage stopped every night at a different hotel. It was quite expensive to travel such a long way. People had two choices, they could travel inside or outside the carriage. Outside was cheaper, but people often fell off

Roads and Canals

Most of the roads in Britain in Jane Austen's time had been built by the Romans. They were in a terrible state, especially in autumn and winter, when there had been a lot of rain or snow. At the beginning of the nineteenth century, a Scottish engineer, called Thomas Telford, built a lot of new roads in England and Wales, so things began to improve. A lot of the new roads were called *turnpikes** and you had to pay to use the road. Because the roads were so bad, canals were often used for transporting things, although people didn't usually travel by canal.

Travelling in the city

In cities like London or Bath, travelling in large carriages was very impractical. Gentlemen often drove small open carriages with one or two horses. In the city centre, sedan chairs were very popular. They were a little bit like modern taxis, except that the chair was carried by two men. They sometimes ran very fast.

Holidays

Holidays were just beginning to be popular amongst the gentry in Jane Austen's day. In *Pride and Prejudice*, Lydia Bennet goes to Brighton, showing that people sometimes went to the seaside.
It was quite normal for people to swim in the sea, although they used bathing machines to take them into the water. This was so that men and women could swim separately.
Aristocratic men often travelled abroad, it was quite normal for young men to travel in France, Italy and Germany when they had finished their education. They were often away on their *Grand Tour* for about a year.

Task • Internet research

Do some research on the Internet about travel and transport in your country. Think about roads, canals, the different means of transport and holidays.

____

____

____

____

____

____

turnpike a road people had to pay to use

TEST YOURSELF

1 **How much can you remember about the story? Answer the questions true (T) or false (F). Correct the false answers.**

		T	F
1	Mrs Bennet wants her daughters to get married.	☐	☐
2	Everyone thinks that Mr Darcy is very shy.	☐	☐
3	Mrs Bennet is a very intelligent woman.	☐	☐
4	Jane is kind to everyone.	☐	☐
5	Mr Collins is a doctor.	☐	☐
6	Mr Bingley falls in love with Jane Bennet.	☐	☐
7	Mr Wickham is a very rich man.	☐	☐
8	Caroline Bingley is very nice about the Bennet family.	☐	☐
9	Mr Wickham marries Lydia Bennet.	☐	☐
10	Jane and Mary get married at the end of the story.	☐	☐

2 **Read this information about Pride and Prejudice. There are ten mistakes. Find them and correct them.**

Pride and Prejudice was written by William Shakespeare. It's the story about the people in the Bennet family, their friends and their lives. Mr and Mrs Bennet have got five sons and they want to make sure they all get married. The heroine of the story is Caroline Bingley. The hero of the story is Mr Collins. At the beginning of the story, Mr Bingley invites everyone to a horse race at Netherfield. At the end of the story, Mr Bingley marries Charlotte Lucas. One of the characters in the story is Lady Catherine de Bourgh. She is always very polite to everyone. Another important character is Mr Wickham. Mr Darcy likes him very much. Unfortunately, Mr Wickham goes to Brighton and kills Lydia. At the end of the story, Elizabeth Bennet and Mr Darcy die in a tragic accident.

3 Choose the best answer – A, B or C for each question.

1 Four couples get married in the story. Who are they?

A Mr Bingley and Charlotte Lucas. Mr Collins and Lady Catherine de Bourgh. Mr Darcy and Caroline Bingley. Mr Bennet and Mrs Bennet. ☐

B Mr Collins and Charlotte Lucas. Mr Wickham and Lydia Bennet. Mr Bingley and Jane Bennet. Mr Darcy and Elizabeth Bennet. ☐

C Mr Collins and Lydia Bennet. Mr Wickham and Charlotte Lucas. Mr Bingley and Elizabeth Bennet. Mr Darcy and Jane Bennet. ☐

2 Which statements best describe the Bennet sisters?

A Jane is serious. Elizabeth is lively. Mary is musical. Kitty and Lydia are calm. ☐

B Jane is kind. Elizabeth is intelligent. Mary is studious. Kitty and Lydia are silly. ☐

C Jane is polite. Elizabeth is calm. Mary is funny. Kitty and Lydia are boring. ☐

3 What does Elizabeth feel about marriage?

A That it's important for her to find a rich husband with a large house. ☐

B That she'll only marry someone she can love and respect. ☐

C That marriage isn't important for her. ☐

4 What pastimes were common at the time of the story?

A Riding, fishing, jogging, writing letters and telling jokes. ☐

B Gardening, writing letters, walking, cooking and photography. ☐

C Reading, drawing, writing letters, music and dancing. ☐

4 Did you like the story of Pride and Prejudice? Why/Why not?

I liked/didn't like the story of Pride and Prejudice because _______

____

____

____

____

____

____

____

____

SYLLABUS

Level B1

This reader contains the items listed below as well as those included in Levels A1 and A2.

Nouns:
complex noun phrases.

Verbs:
present perfect simple: unfinished past with for and since, recent past with just, Past Perfect Simple, reported speech, used to, should for obligation, would for hypothesis and polite requests, must for deduction, may for possibility.

Types of Clause:
type-two conditionals, conditionals with unless, clauses with although, clauses with so...that, time clauses with as soon as, until, before and after.